My Life After Hate reminds all of us who are educators of the need to make each student feel valued and to provide a sense of belonging to our young people. Arno's story implores us to develop relationships with young people, to hear their hard questions, and to help them make sense of a complex and at times contradicting world. This is an inspirational story that reminds us that we can grow, we can change, we can transcend and overcome our past!"

—Dimitry Anselme, former H.S. Teacher & Principal, Director of Program Staff Development at Facing History & Ourselves

"*My Life After Hate* is for anyone who thinks that change is impossible or too difficult. Arno's honest look into his past as a white power skinhead and his long journey out of hatred is proof that change is possible in the unlikeliest places. This book is for anyone who underestimates their own power to transform their life or feels they lack the courage to reach out to others they once feared."

—Lisa Kaiser, Journalist, Shepherd Express

"Society discusses hate and diversity in sterilized language; this book tells the story first hand. Be prepared to be riveted, intrigued and shocked. An astonishing ride through a dark world of violence and the process of rehabilitation."

—Amber Miller, M.B.A., Wisconsin Women's Business Initiative

"It's not so uncommon for those who have gone astray in ways that harm others to eventually get onto a more humane path. What's extraordinary about Arno Michaels is his dedication to the larger enterprise of fighting bigotry and the destructive violence that often grows from it. *My Life After Hate* is an illuminating window into the origins of this repentant man's mission."

—Will Fellows, Author of *Gay Bar*, **Co-Creator of the Shall Not Be Recognized project**

"Arno, you have helped me with myself more then you'll ever know… as I read the book I can light a cig, lay back, close my eyes and picture myself in nearly all the same situations. The situations that you had found yourself in I know are true and accurate and not fabricated or exaggerated. The stories I've heard before, many years back from some of the same people you talk about in the book. I just wanna say thank you for all your hard work, it has made it easier for a person like me to move along with my life. The last ten years have been spent withdrawn and stand-offish with people. Reality was out of step with what I'd considered reality—a stranger in a strange land kinda feeling. With the old days and old ways behind me, I had no idea how to fit in with my new world…"
—Rob, former white power skinhead

"My son Preston (11 years of age) finished your book. We talked every night about what he had read and what he thought about it. I answered any questions he had to the best of my ability and then I asked him some questions… when asked his favorite part of the book he immediately responded 'Charlie Dee's English 201; the part when he read his essay in the small group, that was love, compassion and forgiveness—and he felt it.' I also asked him what he thought of chapter 4 (lead pipe), and if he felt it was necessary for the book. He paused to think for a moment and then replied, 'It shows you who he really was and what he was really thinking or not thinking at that point in his life… without it we wouldn't know how far he has come. It's real, it was his life, and he was brave enough to share it with us.'"
—Laura Bielefeldt, Full-Time Mom

authentic presence

PUBLICATIONS

My Life After Hate
Copyright © 2012 Arno Michaelis

LCCN: 2010916629
ISBN: 978-0-9831290-9-7
Printed in the United States of America
Third Edition: December 2012

Cover Design: Arno Michaels   Cover Art: Bashir Malik
Editor: Tanya Cromartie

Authentic Presence Publications
544 E Odgen Ave · Suite 700-260 · Milwaukee, WI · 53202

Minnijean Brown-Trickey, one of "The Little Rock Nine" who led the Civil Rights movement as a teenager defying school segregation in 1957, holding a copy of *My Life After Hate* given to her by Memorial High School Senior Eric Wells in Eau Claire, Wisconsin.

contents

forewords:

Asked to contribute a foreword to Arno Michaels' *My Life After Hate*, my first thought was to sing his praises. To tell the world what a wonderful person he has become. Thankfully, it dawned on me instead to share what I have gained from Life After Hate (LAH). Naturally, the reader of this book will have an appreciation of Arno's story of transformation and his discovery of basic human goodness. However, the true power and purpose of his story lives within Life After Hate, the magazine, for it is a vehicle of compassion in action.

For over a decade I have worked to turn the tide of violence, oppression, and ethnic exclusion in Milwaukee, Wisconsin. Through my organization, The Summer of Peace Initiative, I have worked to the point of exhaustion to empower and train teens and young adults as community advocates and agents of peace. It wasn't until I stumbled upon lifeafterhate.org that I realized my passion was lost and my strategy shaky and weak.

We had been fighting for peace. What hypocrisy. What contradiction. I commented on one of Arno's articles in the first issue of LAH, never expecting a response. I had become used to people not responding to me and my internet inquiries. Arno responded. We talked on the phone for a long time. I listened. I doubted. I hated. I stereotyped. Yet, I felt a deep curiosity about the mission of his organization, so I set up a meeting with him.

I was nervous about meeting an ex-white supremacist. As a black woman, I experienced apprehension and fear as a matter of course. Never mind the fact that I had been teaching diversity and tolerance to my students. Before our meeting I researched him. I googled him. I studied the magazine. I obsessively stared at his photos, searching his face for information. What information? I did not know. I told my daughter I had a meeting with a former racist. She responded with concern and doubt. "Mom, what if he isn't really reformed and he is just setting you up to hurt you or something." That thought crossed my mind also. But the content and tone of the magazine dismissed the thought, as I had come to feel the genuine apology coursing through its pages.

Life After Hate has spent the last year working with my organization. Through LAH's Community Outreach programming, The Summer of Peace Initiative has become stronger and deeper in pursuit of our goal. Life After Hate has enabled me to re-ignite the fire which burned so fiercely when I founded Summer of Peace Initiative ten years ago. My students have come to love Arno Michaels and his mission, as he loves them. It warms my heart to see our black and brown youth high fivin' with Arno as he walks through the door. They listen to his words and understand the goals of Life After Hate, the magazine, and the curriculum. They experienced peace in themselves through LAH's yoga workshops. They gained teamwork and communication skills through LAH's Rock Climbing workshops. Initially, as a director of my own program, I was jealous to see how engaged my students were with Arno. Over time I learned to appreciate the gifts LAH has blessed my program with. Most of all, I embrace whole-heartedly the gift of contributing to LAH and its mission.

After attending LAH's workshops a few times, my daughter said something so sweet. She asked, "Is Arno going to be at the next leadership meeting?" I replied with a tinge of jealousy, "Why?" "Because I like being friends with somebody who used to hate me!"

The following is an affirmation I created for myself. It was wholly inspired by my journey with lifeafterhate.org, its contributors, staff, and readers.

I have the power to do something different. Feel something safer. Think something better. Be genuinely nicer. Live my day brighter. Because hope is in my heart. The knowledge is in my mind. And compassion for my human family is in my soul.

-Tanya Cromartie
Director, Summer of Peace Initiative, Milwaukee

In January of 2007, I was about 8 months out of a five-year long abusive relationship. In my painful emotional state, I was trying desperately to move on and move forward. I found the feelings and self-reflection and aloneness alternately unbearable and necessary. I struggled to remain still in those sensations, as if it were bondage meant to keep me from some addictive substance. In my weaker moments, I thought I could no longer endure being alone with my thoughts and self, and the reality of the hard work I would have to undertake to change my world. I looked through websites like Yahoo! Personals and Match.com. I man-shopped. Because having a man would fix this for me, right? Cognitively, I was smarter than that, but behaviorally, I can't deny what my instinctive reactions reflected about my secret beliefs. I was still quite capable of bullshitting myself in those days. Those of us who get caught up in any self-destructive behavior, whether it is drugs, alcohol, hate, or relationships with people who hurt us, must keep a constant vigilance over our thought patterns.

What I found on those websites wasn't that impressive. Mostly men in mid-life crises who were fresh out of marriages that they got into without thinking about it too deeply in the first place, men who were still in the throes of their newly rediscovered freedom yet also longing for the comfort of a steady woman to care for them. Men at the mercy of their drastically shifting whims and emotions who could not or would not take the first step in understanding themselves. Nobody to whom I'd trust my vulnerable heart and tenuous position in life. As much as I secretly wished for a man to save me, I also knew all too well that the wrong man could make life hell.

After months of finding nothing to get my panties in a twist over, I came across the profile of a guy who was cute in an off-beat way and had the best-written, most unique and compassionate profile I'd ever seen. He listed his turn-ons and they had nothing to do with sex. They had everything to do with life and love and humanity. I wrote to him and we found a lot in common; our sense of the world, our sense of fairness, and our sense of possibility. He shared openly about his past as a white power skinhead but was afraid I would condemn him for it. As a person who tries to understand every kind of person, I welcomed the process of learning from his experiences. We were very excited about our connection and each intoxicated on the awesomeness of the other.

After a week or two of this, we decided to have a date. On Cinco de Mayo, we met for Mexican food, a walk by Lake Michigan, and then headed back to my apartment to make a tres leches cake (which was awful, but in my defense, I'm only part-Mexican). As much honest-to-goodness, wholesome fun as we had in each other's company, the romance aspect of it wasn't gelling, even though it seemed we were both willing it to. I didn't understand, so I tried to ignore the issue and focus on the fact that I wanted someone who was so good and so fun in my life.

A few days after our date, he called and confessed that it wasn't the right time for him to have a relationship. He was still heartbroken over his previous girlfriend—struggling with a rollercoaster of emotions and he liked and respected me too much to subject me to it. It felt like a rejection and I was disappointed, but I put on my best smile and with a smiling voice told him I understood. I thanked him for being upfront enough to not take me on that emotional ride. Then I hung up the phone and cried, just a little.

My girlfriend called to ask about it all after I'd had enough time to formulate my official stance on the outcome. I said, like a big girl, "Just because I'm ready for an Arno doesn't mean the world owes me one."

Over the years, the nature of our relationship and love has become clearer. The path we took lead to something bigger than anything it could have become had we continued to date each other. An attempt at a romantic relationship probably wouldn't have amounted to anything other than a disappointing mediocrity, because it would have been a forced and pathetic coupling of two broken people trying their best to not break each other or themselves any further—and inevitably failing.

We always kept in touch and kept tabs on each other's projects and changes in life, once in a while meeting for dinner as friends. It was true that I had never met anyone like him, or him me, and the same has been true since. Arno has a viewpoint on things that I can't get from anyone else.

Last year I was contemplating leaving a cushy job that I had upended my life to land to start my own business in an unstable economy. Everyone was telling me, quite logically, that I was insane. People were genuinely afraid for me. I needed someone who would tell me it was a great idea and go balls to the wall with it. So I called Arno. He did not fail me.

In fact, he sweetened the deal.

He told me about his new endeavor: a monthly online magazine dedicated to promoting basic human goodness and diversity appreciation. He invited me to write for it and I gladly accepted. As the project progressed, it was clear he was going to need all hands on deck, so I threw myself into it with love not only for Arno but also for the mission. We put out our first issue as co-editors on January 18th, 2010, the Dr. Martin Luther King Jr. Holiday, and are fast approaching our first anniversary issue. As I've seen the sincerity behind every decision he makes for the organization and the complete calm with which he approaches every person who doubts his change of heart, I've come to realize just how special a person Arno Michaels is, and just what an important role he has in the future of race relations in America and abroad.

Since launching the online magazine, opportunities to reach out to people affected by violence have zoomed at us from every direction. We get e-mails from people touched by the magazine content who are looking to change their lives as well. Arno mentors teens in the Summer of Peace Initiative, a Milwaukee-based movement to instill in kids a sense of self-worth and community engagement, whose founder Tanya has become a friend and mentor to our organization. He does public speaking, sharing his story to persuade others to walk away from violence and toward love for the human race. Through my SpeakUP & SpeakOUT project, Life After Hate has touched the lives of many women by providing them a forum. They use their voice by sharing writing about domestic violence. Some just come and listen. We have writing workshops and many other collaborative projects in the works also.

As a result of falling into each other's lives and having the grace to recognize how we could most be loving and useful to one another, Arno and I have not only figured out how to love ourselves and other people, and to change our own destinies, but also how to invite each and every one of you to do the same.

In the years since that Cinco de Mayo date, I mastered the impulse to fall back on a man, acquired the new impulse to run from all of them, and then mastered that impulse, too. Arno moved past the self-doubt that stood in his way and now we stand, shoulder to shoulder, as kind warriors teaching others how to love others by loving themselves. We encounter people every day who find the courage to pull themselves up and out of dark, desolate holes because we have the courage to talk about how we got out of ours. We come together for family suppers with our significant others, children, and Life After Hate brothers and sisters and marvel at how those tentative first steps turned into next steps, and how each subsequent footfall brought us miles from where we started. Our hearts thrill to think of where the next steps will lead.

You're invited to join us on our journey. ..

-Angie Aker
Co-Editor, Life After Hate

arno michaelis

for my mom
my dad
my little brother
my aunt Geri and uncle Bob
my grandparents

and most of all
for my daughter

arno michaelis

my life after hate

(In the interest of privacy, names and identifying characteristics of some individuals have been changed.)

1: dolor

Discussing the horrendous things I've done is a painful process. When I feel pain, I'm prone to lashing out. Early drafts of this were rife with jabs at people who had nothing to do with the story of me being a skinhead. I'd just as soon not tell you this, but I feel obliged to do so because it reveals that I'm still struggling with my anger.

I have so much to learn in order to heal. I need people to listen to me. I need to listen to them to facilitate such learning, and damn the scabs if tearing them off is part of the healing process.

But how much of that discomfort is caused by the lens through which my past is examined? The pain in question flares when I relive things that I'm horrified I've done. Hurt that hurt made can propagate if we're unable to let it pass.

Human beings will never be free from pain, nor should we ever be. Pain is an invaluable teacher as well as a builder of character and vehicle of spiritual growth. But not all pain is necessary, or necessarily constructive. We can acknowledge the painful nature of life and embrace the opportunity it presents. The "good pain" can be sorted from the bad. The pain of others can be soothed. Or we can remain in constant and futile flight from pain with no regard for who gets trampled along the way.

It would be a constructive process if I could learn

from the pain itself. By tweaking the focus of the lens, I can learn how to recognize the occasions when pain is necessary and how to make better choices in the future. So often I find myself getting upset about things that aren't important. The situation worsens as ire saps available energy for things that are vital. Thought, love, and empathy gird against pain, making it much easier to endure and examine.

That's one of many crucial lessons that are finally starting to take root for me. When we are hurt by whatever, we should be patient and thoughtful and learn from the experience instead of simply making other people hurt. So easy to say, yet difficult to deliver—at least in the beginning. Once the nourishment of constructively coping with pain is realized, the process becomes consistently easier and more rewarding. Life After Hate isn't a how-to—I recommend a good yoga class and meditation practice for that—but it certainly is cathartic. And I hope thought-provoking and conversation-inspiring.

I had lost my mind for a good long stretch. Compassion brought me back as it was given to me and as I learned to give it back. Please talk about the mindless things I've done with your friends—or better yet, perceived enemies. We've all done mindless things, but also smart things, and amazing things. Let's share our experiences with honest openness and see if we can help each other out in the process.

2: why

Why Life After Hate? To help people learn to set aside their prejudices and embrace differences.

Being a guy with an imposing presence and a lot of tattoos, I face more prejudice than most white people. I realize that I'm a bit of an eyesore. But beyond the surprised first glances, my appearance tends to evoke vibes of fear, disgust, disdain. People have corralled their young children at the sight of me, as if I'm likely to eat them. The other day an old man stood glaring at me and shaking his head as if I were a mangy stray dog who had just shit on the floor of the grocery store. Even though all of my skinhead ink has been well covered, there are those who still pre-judge me as being a racist. Within a span of seconds, many people make up their minds that the world would be a better place if I weren't in it.

But I volunteered for my tattoos.

You don't volunteer for a skin color.

I'll never truly understand what it's like to be anyone but a white man in the United States. For all of my self-imposed distance from the status quo, I'll never be able to get my head around being the product of generations of hardship. The most brutal chattel slavery in human history. I'll never comprehend being penned up in an impoverished reservation on land that was once sovereign domain. I'll never know how it feels to be denied because of the color of your skin or because of where you came from. To have to watch your children suffer the same fate.

But I still try to understand—by studying the history that the victors didn't write, and interacting with my fellow human beings. Finding out what their favorite color is. Asking what they daydreamed about as a child. Sharing laughs. Discovering the person.

I hope that after someone reads Life After Hate, they'll think twice before pre-judging people for whatever reason. Had you the misfortune of crossing my path 20 years ago, I probably would have garnered an instant and condemning prejudgment. But I changed for the better.

If there can be hope for me, there can be hope for anyone. And considering that I have brothers and sisters who personally made the journey in and out of hate along with me, I know my story isn't a fluke. Each one of us got in, and out, for our own reasons. Some of those reasons were similar, but each story is unique.

Why? Because I need to learn how to best tell my story.

My original idea was to speak in the voice of the time, the voice of a hate-crazed zealot who was perpetually in the process of convincing himself and others that all outside his race must die to save his own. Speaking in that voice, I intended to describe scenes that in the moment were downright good times. Scenes that make me wonder how the same person who acted in them could be the one writing about them today. Did I ever pause for a second then to think that someday I would vomit once I knew what I was doing? That I would cry? I faintly recall whispers of *don't do this...don't hurt them...* coming from somewhere long ago in my soul. But each plea was literally drowned in suds of Huber and Miller and Old Style until the junk thrill of combat thundered once again.

Between benders I immersed myself in racist dogma, taking in only information that supported the tenuous premise that the white race was at once mighty and fragile, and in dire need of conservation by any means necessary. And there is plenty of such information out there if you choose to spin it that way; blacks and Latinos commit crimes, Jews make movies and own banks—you do the math.

It seems simplistic to the point of absurdity to even type such statements now, even though they are technically facts, because now I understand that there is so much value in looking beyond just face value. But back then those were talking points that I would employ to either fire you up to the point where you wanted to knock someone's teeth out or alternately knock yours out for you if you didn't like what I had to say.

It is extremely difficult for me to open the crypts of my past and parade the fucked-up things therein in a way that gets the feeling of those dark times across. Nightmares of smashed skulls and straight razors plague what little sleep I get when I'm immersed back in the days of boots, beer, and blood—utterly horrified by things I used to find glorious comfort in and then horrified again by that. If I can barely write the stuff, who the hell is going to want to read it?

I'm that guy who doesn't know how to act. Who doesn't understand why people run screaming in terror when he thinks he's doing something nice. The image of Frankenstein's monster trying to give the little girl a flower comes to mind, as does the observation that what is intense and scary to most people seems normal and comforting to me. So be advised that *My Life After Hate* is merely a glimpse of the monster that I was, and that it hurts me even more than it hurts you. *My Life After Hate* is basically a reflection on my past in my present-day nice-guy voice. There are a few brushes with the old Arno in the mix to keep it interesting.

Maybe someday I'll write a proper memoir…

Most of all though, *My Life After Hate* is my apology to the world.

In 1988, I was a founding member of what went on to become the largest white power skinhead organization on Earth. In 2007, over a decade since I came to my senses, I was approached by a German skinhead online who said that although he knew I was no longer active in the movement, I was still "in good standing." He offered me a trip to Europe where he had musicians who would serve as my band for a few Centurion shows. Centurion, my former "hate metal" group that sold over 20,000 CDs worldwide by the mid-nineties and who knows how many more since then, was apparently still quite popular with the disgruntled-European-white-kid demographic. Popular enough to make it worth their while to fly me over there. I never replied. Until now.

As nice as it would be to just forget about who I was, Centurion alone implores that I make an effort to counteract the damage I've done. People all over the world are inspired to fear one another by my bellowing voice as I type this. I can hardly fade into my successful career as an information technology consultant when the Arno of two decades ago is still busy causing harm.

It's time to break the silence.

It's time for everyone who listens to lyrics I wrote and shouted telling them to hurt innocent people to know that I've somehow lived to regret everything I said. Everyone I hurt.

I don't want them to suffer the same regret. I know where racists are coming from, and I pity them as much as I pity their victims. Hate takes a terrible toll on life. Fear is indeed the mind-killer. We all have the option of living a life of love and compassion, and I'm here to say that the world really is as beautiful a place as you care to envision.

You will find what you're looking for, so think deeply about what it is you seek.

That's why.

arno michaelis

3: how

It's going to be very hard to understand that everything made sense to me back then. It all made sense as it was happening—for the most part I guess. But what about the nice old black lady at McDonald's who asked about the swastika tattoo on my hand and I said, "Aww… it's nothing", inspiring my roommate to bust me out when we got back home? What about the black and Latino guys I worked with printing t-shirts? What would my skinhead friends have said if they saw me laughing and joking with them on coffee breaks? So there were moments when the good in me was dragging my feet. It happened pretty much whenever I'd have extended contact with people who I shouldn't have according to racist dogma—"non-white" people. If I spent any time with them—even the lady at McDonald's who always seemed to be the one taking my order for the weekly payday Big Mac feast—then I would have trouble being mean to them. Hating them. So I would go back to my blinders and close my world off, limiting my experience to pro-white whites only, and input to racist information only.

Did I always know in the back of my mind, at the bottom of my heart, that I was wrong? Or did I truly believe in racial holy war? How about a little of both? Is that possible? Can you be so committed to something so fucked up and go about that business with passion and fervor—for years—while having doubts?

There were so many who dabbled. People who got a glimpse or three, then wussed-out or wised-up. Why couldn't I have moved on? I'm so fucking transient in other aspects of life. Can't work the same job, have the same girlfriend, hobbies, look, etc, for more than a year or two. How did I come to be such an asshole for 7 years? Maybe because I was good at it. Because people followed me and approved of me.

The thing is, I would have been good at whatever I got into. I know that now—not sure if I knew it then. I know I was a cocky jerk who knew he was exceptional. But there wasn't a whole lot of sense of self-preservation. There was plenty of self-destruction though, and I was mostly laughing while it went off. The typical self-centered goals of a young Midwestern white man were absent. I had no interest in McMansions, Rolexes, or Range Rovers. I just liked to get fucked up and fuck things and other people up.

Maybe I was looking for something to believe in when the planets aligned to set me down that path. I was drawn to racist ideology because I felt like white people were getting shafted. We were the underdogs. It was us against the world in an epic battle for forever. Such romance! Getting back in that moment, the taint we cast upon reality definitely had that saga feel. And that was by design. Hitler did it with the torch-lit ceremony and iconic swastika. It felt like you were Beowulf, Siegfried, and Conan all rolled into one. Just a big fucking game of Dungeons & Dragons, till death and prison inevitably show up. Then the shit is real. Then comes the real challenge, the true test of will. Do you back down then? Are you a coward? Or just a fool? That's when you gather all the suffering you can endure and produce and you devour it, because it's the only thing that nourishes you anymore. And you let that fire rage on till it's all you can see. You damn well can't see how burnt and disfigured it makes you—how it scorches your life. It's impossible to see how the hurt you emanate feels on the receiving end, because you have no empathy for other humans. Even your own crew is barren of empathy for each other. You would die for your brothers and sisters, but you are unable to put yourself in their shoes. You don't really care about or understand their individual hopes and dreams, because like you, they have none outside of the movement. Your feeling for them is one of primal pack-mentality. Survival melded with a perverted sense of honor that won't permit you to suffer insult to them any more than to yourself.

Yeah, there were issues at home; dysfunction that paled in comparison to the billions of people on this planet with real problems that was nevertheless catastrophic to me. But looking back I don't see any valid excuse for how fucked-up I turned out.

In the movies I would have been physically beaten by parents and/or ghetto thugs while clawing out survival from an impoverished hovel, like many of my comrades were to one degree or another. But in real life I grew up in a nice house in a nice neighborhood and never went hungry or took a beating. My parents loved me dearly, but that made my dad's drinking and their subsequent fighting a constant hurt that drove me to lash out, denying their love for me and filling that void with hate.

In the absence of love's light, hate can be exciting, seductive. It beckons you and sends torrid, empty power coursing through your veins. At first you think you can dabble. Just for kicks. Just a bit of entertainment to ripple the excruciating monotony of your disdain for the world. You blink, and you're covered in someone's blood. Another blink and the doors of your cell are slamming shut. A blink later and the image of your best friend's mannequin-looking corpse as cold and wooden and wrong as the open casket it sits in is seared into your brain forever. You rub your eyes in response to the blinks and the tears of your family run down your face. The tears of the parents of the people you battered beyond recognition. The tears of survivors who feel their children torn from their arms and their parents murdered all over again at the sight of you.

That's how it happens… how it happened to me, at least.

Once when I was a kid some friends and I were playing with matches in a parched summer field. We set an anthill on fire and found ourselves hypnotized by the ruthless spread of the flame, then dancing and whooping as the entire meadow was engulfed. The damage and consequence of our actions didn't occur to us until the roar of a fire-truck doused our revelry with that panicked realization of, "Holy shit. *What have I done?*"

arno michaelis

4: lead pipe

"I've had it with that fucking mouse."
"It's a rat, dude. ...I'm pretty sure it's a rat."

I sat on a dilapidated couch in-between Clayton and Pat, forming a trio of shaven heads further uniformed by steel-toed Doc Martin boots and flight jackets. In front of us was an old-school, dresser-sized console television. The TV only had one channel, which was whatever the rodent in the terrarium that had taken the place of the picture tube was doing at the moment. There was a time when we had cable, but it was shut-off when beer money was deemed a priority over paying the cable bill. Just to make sure Time-Warner Cable knew I wasn't fucking around, I had kicked-out the tube sometime in the preceding blur. That was great fun at the time, but when the dust and shards of glass settled, we realized how much we missed having something utterly meaningless to stare at, hence the rat-cage.

I had just returned from the sand-nigger-mart on the corner where I had procured a pack of Newport 100s and a 40-ounce bottle of Red Bull malt liquor for myself, and a pack of Winstons and a can of Coke for Pat. Clayton was somehow more penniless than Pat and me and was thus left to scavenge butts from the ashtray and hope for some kind of beer windfall later in the evening. The stale ingrained stench of beer and tobacco freshened for the moment as I cracked my 40 and fired up a niggerette, making sure to cut a celtic cross into the filter first in a mindless ritual of defiance. Any time I got shit for smoking menthol, which was constantly, I would point out that any commonality with blacks was nullified by my thumbnailed brand of white pride. There wasn't anything I could do to purify the malt liquor, but that particular contradiction was lost in wanton drunken violence along with everything else.

The rundown house we were sitting in at 700 E. Wright St. was nicknamed "The 700 Club." We all derived great amusement at the idea of our rapidly deteriorating den of debauchery sharing a moniker with that shitbag Jesus-nut scam on TV—the ones that still had picture tubes at least. Visitors were assailed upon arrival for heartfelt donations in our namesake's honor, but we felt we were more forthright about the future use of such monies (beer), than 'ol Pat Robertson was.

Pat O'Malley and I lived at The 700 Club with Clayton and a dwindling number of punk rockers who were systematically being driven out via plagues and horrors such as the thoughtless eating of their vegetarian hotdogs. As the punk rockers fled, we would shoe-in one of a long list of hovering transient skinheads to take their place. The rat/mouse/whatever-it-was that lived in the TV belonged to Mike McQueen, one of the last surviving punk rockers we were hellbent to displace. On

Pat's lap was a kitten that my crazy cat-lady aunt had just given to me. We had lovingly named him "Bully", after learning that British skinheads sometimes referred to themselves as "Bully Boys."

"How fast do you think Bully would kill the rat?" Pat wondered.

"Shit, one minute and it gets its neck broke." I said.

Clayton begged to differ. "I dunno. Bully's just a kitten."

Pat was unimpressed. "He's gonna fuck up the rat like I'm gonna fuck you up!"

"Heh! Only one way to find out, huh Paddy O?" I chuckled, amused by the prospect of changing the channel so-to-speak..

"You know it bro..." and Pat got up to put the cat in the mouse cage. The three of us watched intently to see Bully catch the rat in his mouth, then shake it in an efficient neck-breaking motion. Howling in approval and focused on the aftermath, we were surprised by the door opening as our roommate Brian walked in with John, a bunch of his West Bend crew, and a wicked-cold blast of Wisconsin winter air.

Brian wasn't necessarily a punk rocker, but he wasn't a skinhead like we were either. He was one of the original members of our 700 Club, a bit older than we were, and more than a bit jaded and elitist about his personal history in the Milwaukee counter-culture scene. He had this fucked-up notion that you could be a skinhead and not be white power. That was the root of more and more disagreements as Pat and I changed the complexion of The 700 Club from a punk-infused collective to a swastika-flying skinhead headquarters. We had outlived our own punk phases over the past year and were busily involved in the transition to a nationwide white racist movement without really understanding what we were getting into. All we knew was that beloved fights happened when walking down the street sporting white power t-shirts and a closely-shaven #1 crop. Blind-drunk on 150-proof hostility, we had finally found the ultimate expression of our hate for society, and we strove to inspire a like hatred in all who would listen.

John and his boys were also a bit on the fence, but seemed to lean toward Pat and me for old-times' sake, since I had been drinking and street-fighting alongside them for a few years by then.

Brian, who liked Bully and didn't really like the rat, got a kick out of the new TV channel. "What the fuck are you guys doing?!" he guffawed. "Holy shit, Queenie's gonna go ballistic! Haha! How long have you been drinking Arno? Jesus Christ."

John was a bit disgusted with our newfound bloodsport but grinning nonetheless. "In other news, apparently there's a hippie house party tonight."

My ears pricked up at the mention of the hippie house. It was a lower flat a few houses north of Pizza Man restaurant on Oakland Avenue, known for its parties. Parties that featured relatively large amounts of beer to drink, pretty girls to bother, and hippies to beat up. A veritable skinhead shangri-la if there ever was one. But we had been summarily banned from setting foot on the property after a window-breaking incident that went down a few weeks earlier.

"They'll call the cops the minute we get there. It's too cold for that shit."

Brian replied, "We just saw Cindy on Downer, and she said it's cool and that they're gonna have a few barrels. We just can't break anything."

"And they're gonna have barrels." John added.

Pat was already lacing up his boots. "That Cindy wants my cock. You assholes should all be glad I'm such a fucking stud or you wouldn't have anything to drink tonight."

I slammed the rest of my 40 and belched as I coaxed another Newport from the pack and fired it up. Clayton freed Bully from the late rodent's abode and set him on the couch to savor his meal.

John had brought a 12 of Meister Brau with him that we felt obliged to finish before we left, but only after verifying that we collectively had enough money to get more beer on the way for later on. The 9 p.m. beer curfew in Milwaukee had ingrained upon us the necessity of planning ahead for beer, if nothing else in our lives. Over the short time we had been lacing up and downing the Meister Brau, our crew had swelled to almost 20, and the witching hour of 9 p.m. was upon us.

I let rip another robust burp and called the mission to order by calling shotgun in John's Chevette.

"You ain't outside yet punk!" Pat laughed as he checked me into the door on his way past.

We piled as many people as possible into John's car and the rusted-out VW Fox belonging to the chubby girl who we let hang around only because she had a car and would occasionally cough up some beer money. There was a brutal wind whipping through the city that December night in 1987, the kind that tears at every area of exposed skin and stuffs a large number of skinheads into two smallish cars in a matter of seconds. Pat and I traded blows as we scrambled for the car door. We settled for both squeezing into the front seat after the back had been stuffed with our comrades. A hand poked out from the pile in the back holding out a battered cassette marked "Oi!" in black magic marker. A muffled voice, presumably that of the hand's owner, said "Pop this shit in man—" and Pat maneuvered his torso enough to oblige.

Following the clack into the tape deck was a banging of bar chords and simple yet frenetically powerful drumbeats that conjured the thickly accented voice of some very pissed-off British guy who proclaimed "...*get out of our way or get took for a ride...we've just got violence, IN OUR MINDS!!*" John's car shook and rolled as we all rocked out to the extent that the cramped quarters would allow and shouted along in agreement. The combination of body heat and car heat took the bite off the chill by the time we had traveled the six blocks out of Riverwest and crossed the bridge over the Milwaukee River to the East Side, where the college bars and generally more interesting scenes existed.

"Goddammit John, it's almost NINE!" I didn't even have a watch or really know what time it was, but my drunky-sense told me that NINE O'CLOCK was treacherously near, and the prospect of not having a case of beer to drink later on loomed heavy on my soul.

Screeching to a halt outside Open Pantry, John admonished me, "Settle down man! Look, your boyfriend's even working tonight. I bet he would totally sell you beer any time for a shot at that fine ass of yours."

Raucous laughter erupted from the peanut gallery as I reached around Pat's head to slap the back of John's, then fell out of the car as Pat opened the door. The gay guy was working. He never knew what to make of me when I went in there with pockets full of nickels and dimes to exchange for cases of Huber (The Skinhead War Beer). I was openly hostile to him, as I was to any faggots I came across, but I always stopped short of really fucking with him as long as I got my beer. I think he just didn't want any trouble and thus put up with my blatantly underage alcohol purchases rather than find out what would happen if he carded me. Or maybe he just wanted me to drink myself to death, which I was clearly doing at the tender age of 17. Just to keep the queer in line, I glared at him as I passed the counter and bee-lined for the beer coolers. In a flash, and with my eyes on the Marlboro clock that indicated a time of 8:57 p.m., I plunked three twelve packs of Huber in front of the register and began the arduous process of hauling enough change and tattered singles out of my pockets to settle up.

"Not AGAIN," sighed the faggot clerk.

It seemed like he was being extra-femmy on purpose. I really wanted to just reach across the counter and belt him one but knew that a reliable source of beer purchasing was way too valuable to endanger by such trivial but tempting violence.

"It's all money."

"And who has to count it?"

"You, if you wanna get paid for this beer."

"Well, I guess I need the change anyway, when the crackheads come in for the single smokes."

That almost made me crack a smile, which made me shudder to think that I was standing there having a dialogue with a homo. After snowplowing a mountain of change over the counter, I gathered my alcohol and tobacco and hurried off for the door, which was blocked by a couple of entering gangbangers. I paused long enough to catch their eyes and simply said "Nigger" as I stared them down. I figured they must have been aware of the two carloads of my buddies outside, because they just shook their heads and proceeded into the store. I pivoted for a moment, arms full of beer, to make sure they knew that I was happy to oblige if they wanted to fight.

John honked his horn, and I looked out to see Pat shrugging in front of a back seat stuffed with hands, all gesturing for me to go. My thoughts turned back to the hippie house and the possible trifecta of beer, pussy, and knuckles that awaited me there. Getting drunk(er) and getting in a fight would do if I had to settle for 2 out of 3.

I wedged myself back into the front seat, and we drove the remaining three blocks to the hippie house, which was close enough to a very popular intersection to make parking a royal bitch. After circling a few times, John finally gave up on any sort of decent parking place, which left us with another two blocks to sprint to our destination. We might as well have parked at the damn Open Panty. I left the beers in John's car, intending to drink all the hippies' beer and return home to drink mine later on. The rusty VW had parked about as far down another street, and our two half-crews collided to form a whole one and stampede the final half-block to the hippie house itself.

"Holy SHIT, it's cold!!" someone lamented as a platoon of boots and shaven heads thundered onto the front porch.

I was first to the door, so I did the honors of banging on it almost hard enough to break it down in tribute to our common freezing status. Nicole, Cindy's roommate —who not only did not want Pat's cock but who didn't want anything to do with any of us whatsoever—opened the door a crack and peered out from behind the chain.

"Fuck you guys!" she said. "You better leave like fucking yesterday, or I'm calling the cops!"

Pat turned on the Irish charm as best he could while his teeth chattered, "Hey Nicole, Cindy invited us. We'll be cool, I promise! We're turning blue out here, can't we come in for one just to warm up?"

Nicole wasn't having any of it, "Fuck that, Pat; Cindy's not here, and you Nazi scumbags better leave NOW or I'm calling the cops!" And with that, the door slammed shut in my face.

There was a demonstrative securing of the door lock, and we were left on the porch. Not ready to give up our dream of free beer and smutty women despite being firmly shut-down by Nicole, we kept beating on the door as if that would somehow sweeten the deal for them. For a split second, it seemed as if the cop-knocking actually had inspired a change of heart when the door opened a crack. But instead of naked drugged-out hippie girls with multiple frosty mugs of beer in their arms, a lone lead pipe flashed out in a swooping arc that ran perpendicular to my forehead, which instantly busted open as the two objects met. I remember a reverberating "*DONNGGGG!*" sound, like a church bell ringing, then seeing the pipe bounce off my head in slow motion.

Instinctively, I reached up and caught the pipe, forcing my way through the door at the same time. The person who hit me was a little hippie guy. He was quite surprised to find me coming at him, and desperately trying to pull the pipe and himself as far away from me as possible. Holding the pipe in my right hand, I grabbed him by the collar with my left and used his body to force my way into the living room. My boys piled in behind me as the party attendees withdrew. There was a glass coffee table in the living room that I already had my assailant backpedaling toward, so I kicked out his legs and sent him smashing through the table, following him down to land my elbow in his throat with a crunchy thud.

Coughing and gasping, he scrambled up, both hands still on the pipe, refusing to let go. I didn't know if he thought he was going to get another crack at me or if he knew that if I got the pipe I was going to return the favor with it. I was much bigger than him, and consumed with adrenaline and bloodlust, so it took almost no effort for me to throw Little Hippie Guy over the couch and pounce after him. He ended up on the floor, still gulping for air like a displaced goldfish and curled up in a fetal position around the pipe, as if not letting go of the pipe was going to save him somehow. Before he could scurry away, I straddled him, holding his head down by the hair with my left hand and pistoning punches to his face with my right. He was trying to curl his face into his torso to avoid the blows, but I kept yanking his head back by the hair to allow my fist unabated access to his nose, jaw, and eyes.

I had his arms pinned with my right leg and the rest of his body secured by my weight. It took me a few punches to get the optimum range dialed in, but once I did, his nose flattened, along with the rest of his face, which began to give way from the mechanical pounding of my fist. Blood was everywhere. I wasn't aware that the first blood spattering around his face got there by pouring from the gash in my head, but the sight of it propelled me into further frenzy, and soon his blood and my own became indistinguishable. It pooled around us and splashed across the room. I had forgotten about the pipe, effectively blind to all external stimuli, focused on nothing but repeatedly burying my fist deeper and deeper into his head.

Time stood still. I didn't know if 30 seconds or 30 minutes had passed since the church bell rang, but I didn't really care. There was no pain, just delicious rage and the feeling of omnipotence as I exacted revenge. I could feel the pipe-swinger's body squirming in a futile attempt to free himself that grew weaker with each punch I landed. My right arm continued to autonomously fire at his face, long after it was clear that he was no longer a threat. Now my attention turned to what the fuck else was happening to identify any other possible threats. I realized that it wasn't just me and the guy who hit me; there were a bunch of terrified hippie-house denizens shrieking about the house, and my crew of skinheads took great pleasure in inspiring that terror as they took in the righteous beating I was administering. My boys didn't realize how badly I was hurt until they circled around. The laughter of my friends turned to rage as it became apparent that at least half of the blood that painted the room came from the gaping wound in my forehead.

Pat was the first to jump in. *"LOOK WHAT YOU DID TO MY BROTHER, MOTHERFUCKER!!"* he roared, planting a steel-toed kick to Little Hippie Guy's face with all the force he could muster. Nobody fucked with Pat's family, and he and I were closer to each other than we were to our actual siblings. Pat's seventeen years were rife with violence, and all of it went into every kick landed on that sorry son of a bitch.

I adjusted the angle of my own blows to allow Pat's kicks access to his face. The focus of my fist moved to throat and jaw, while Pat's boot punted squarely again and again. The rest of my crew swarmed around and fought among themselves for suitable openings to deliver kicks of their own. Skinheads react as a pack in violent situations. The rest of the guys fed off the fury that had leaped from me to Pat to them like wildfire. We could all feel the group attack; it was as if a single murderous entity had been formed by the initial big bang of the pipe striking my head.

As the intensity of the retaliation peaked, its object had resigned himself to his fate. He had stopped squirming, crying and pleading. But my fist and the boots of my boys kept on going. Little Hippie Guy's friends were powerless to intervene beyond huddling in the corners and shrieking for us to stop. I didn't know if it was too late. The thought occurred to me that the man I was sitting on was going to die. The notion had a clinical detachment to it at first, then zoomed in to a panicked thrill. The guy shouldn't have hit me! *What the fuck was he thinking?!* Everyone on the East Side knows who we are and what we do. Why would he think that there would be any other outcome? As he went limp, the pipe rolled from his grasp, unnoticed by any of us, to his great fortune.

Nicole, however, did notice the pipe. She picked it up, and in a lone showing of hippie courage took a girly, ineffective swing at Pat. The pipe thunked off Pat's back harmlessly, and he turned to address her, grabbing the pipe himself and swinging her around by it.

Finally someone bellowed, "COPS!!" which initiated our withdrawal.

First the flightier members of our squad broke off; the guys who were always on the periphery, never starting or ending fights themselves, but always happy to throw a boot in once it was on. Those guys snapped out of the communal bloodlust pretty quick when alerted to the possibility of police involvement.

John clarified, *"THEY'RE CALLING THE COPS!!"* Not actual cops on the scene just yet, but impending cops. Nonetheless, he saved my assailant's life with his alert.

Most of my crew had fled, leaving Pat and me winding down over the quasi-carcass of the Little Hippie Guy. I was still pounding away, unable to stop.

Finally Pat had to catch my arm and drag me up and off what was left of the pipe-swinger. "We gotta get the fuck out, bro—"

O'Malley was cool and collected despite the preceding chaos, even having the presence of mind to avoid saying my name during a crime-time. Pat had the strange combination of a very short fuse yet uncommon level-headedness under pressure. I snapped out of my berzerk as Pat hauled me up, taking in the scene. The hippie house people were still lamenting, but beginning to de-huddle themselves out of the corners as my guys cleared out. My attacker-turned-victim was a destroyed heap in the center of a sparsely decorated bedroom off of the living room. I noticed the obligatory stench of patchouli mingling with the iron musk of blood, which was everywhere. Radiating from the former guy-with-the-pipe was a bloody supernova, thick and swirling around the area where he lay, becoming more nebulous as it spiraled outward and dispersed about the room in splashes and spatters. The taste of blood was so strong that I felt like I just chugged a big stein mug full.

I turned to Pat as we trotted out "Man, I think I got that kid's blood in my fuckin mouth—" spitting a mouthful on the door.

"It's probly your own blood, dude. Don't worry about it. We gotta get the fuck outta here."

It wasn't until we were piling into John's car to make our getaway that I truly realized my injury's existence. Being a lifelong head-wound collector, I instinctively looked for some sort of material to use to apply pressure to stop the bleeding. My flight jacket would do nicely.

The short ride back to The 700 Club was filled with laughter and excited retelling of kicks and punches. As the adrenaline wore off, my own blood loss began to take its toll, and I was pretty woozy when we got back to the house. I wobbled as I led the way in, a blood-covered illustration of the gory tale that was enthusiastically related by multiple guys to everyone who had missed the action. I was concentrating on getting to the bathroom to wash up and assess the damage to my skull. Our other roommate Pat, who was a bit of a hippie himself and thus proclaimed "Hippie Pat" in distinction from Pat O'Malley, had a girlfriend who was some kind of med student, and she was getting all bent out of shape about me looking in the mirror.

She cried, "Don't let him look in the mirror, HE'LL GO INTO SHOCK!!" which we all thought was hilarious considering that we wallowed in violence regularly.

A flip of the bathroom light revealed my grim countenance in the filmy mirror. There was a gash approximately two inches long and maybe half that wide that had eased bleeding enough to reveal the white of my skull.

"Hey guys! I can see my own skull!!" I announced to the house in much the same manner as a kid announces the discovered contents of a highly anticipated Christmas present.

With a grin that complemented my wound, I emerged from the bathroom to proudly display the bone-showing laceration to admiring compatriots, who rewarded me with an ice-cold Huber that was accepted with true gratitude. There have been countless moments in my life when I was absolutely floored by just how great a beer tasted, and this was certainly one of the top 10. The beer was so delicious, in fact, that drinking about 20 to 30 more of them in succession became a necessity, but the aforementioned girlfriend of Hippie Pat, along with my skinhead brother Pat, prevailed on me to get to the emergency room for some repair. Once they agreed to the condition that I was allowed to bring a supply of Huber along for the ride, I got in Hippie Pat's girlfriend's car, and we headed for St. Mary's Hospital. I think I managed to down two or three more beers along the few miles there. I walked in the ER and went up to the reception desk where a nurse asked my name without looking up from her paperwork.

"Arni Nelson," I replied, dusting off my trusty alias from reserve for occasions such as this.

"And what can we do for you?" she said, still not looking up.

"Well, let's see— For starters, I got this problem with my head—" which prompted a look up from the papers and a subsequent "OH WOW!" from the nurse, who scurried off to bring back a gurney and some ER jockeys to roll me into a room. I'm not sure if time flew because of the pleasant combination of alcohol intake and substantial blood loss or if they were just really on their shit that night in the St. Mary's ER, but the whole process of getting sewn up and sent on my way seemed to whiz by with an impressive quickness. I was back to the car and into another beer in relatively short order.

Back at our house, a full-blown party of our own had manifested. I spent the rest of the evening inhaling beer and alternating between relating the earlier events myself and showing off my stitches while other boot-party attendees related their versions. Miraculously, there was no visit from the police that night or at any other time in regard to the woeful pipe-wielding Little Hippie Guy. Most likely due to drug-related police-wariness on their part, I suspected. In the days that followed, we heard from here and there that the pipe-hitter survived but ended up spending a considerably longer time in the hospital than I did.

The next morning, which for me came in the afternoon, seemed eerily familiar as I sat between Clayton and Pat on the shitty beer-soaked green couch. This time I was a little more hung over, my headache was considerably worse, and now there was literally nothing on TV. It was even shittier without the rodent. I looked over to Pat, who had the cat on his lap again.

"I feel kinda bad about feeding that mouse to Bully . . ."

5: Ann Arbor

Apparently I pissed on Tina and her boyfriend the night before. The armored and barred Detroit bungalow was so packed with skinheads that the kitchen floor was the only place left for them to sleep. According to the testimony of multiple eyewitnesses, I had passed out crumpled in a corner after consuming every last drop of beer in the place, then later arose and took my dick out to swerve about the darkened house as if it would somehow point me to a toilet. Stubbing my boot on Tina's bleach-blonde head, she and the guy (Chris? Eric?) woke just in time to see me standing over them semi-conscious and proceeding to relieve myself in their faces. The testimony continues to reveal that strangely enough, Tina and (Carl?) didn't take kindly to being peed on and were in fact agitated enough to attack me, which they were about to do when Pat awoke to inform them and every other not-from-Milwaukee motherfucker in the house that I piss where ever the fuck I want to and if they didn't like it, we'd beat them to a bloody mess and piss on them again.

There were no takers among the 30 or so other skins who converged in Detroit that weekend to attend the annual rock-throwing festival known as the "Ann Arbor Nazi Rally". All of them instead chose to join Pat in laughing at Tina and whats-his-face as they shed their pissed-up clothes and sleeping bag. Meanwhile, I had stumbled through the basement door and tumbled down the stairs unscathed as only the blind-drunk can. Upon righting myself at the bottom, I shuffled over to the dryer, opened it, and pissed some more on the clothes it contained before collapsing alongside in a pile of lint and empty generic detergent boxes. I awoke sometime when the sun was shining through the heavily barred basement window to the not-so-gentle nudge of Pat's boot.

"Good morning sunshine! Get your drunk ass up. Jane's cooking eggs, you better get some before they piss in yours! Hahaha!"

I grumbled something barely coherent about more beer then allowed myself to be summoned to the kitchen. I didn't remember pissing on Tina and didn't really give a shit when she confronted me about it, shrugging the whole incident off and suggesting that she get to the fucking liquor store to replenish the beer supply.

Our comrades from Detroit, Chicago, and various parts of Ohio had been subjugated by the combination of my drunken barbarism and Pat's strong-armed endorsement of it. They would have followed us to raise a flag on some meaningless numbered Iwo Jima hill amidst a hail of machine gun fire had we chose to lead them there. But instead, after a breakfast of eggs and potatoes (ham, bacon, and/or other meats were foregone to purchase more beer), we piled out of the house in an almost comical clown-car stream to pack into a few vehicles and head for our rendezvous with "The SS Action Group".

As we travelled cross-town in Detroit, I noticed that the vast majority of houses and buildings had plywood or bricks where windows were supposed to be—the ones that weren't burnt-out husks that is. The few places that did have windows were barricaded like Fort Knox in the manner of the house I had just pissed all over. I pointed this out to my crew, explaining that that's what niggers do to a neighborhood and that it was our job to stop them, like an exterminator purging a roach infestation. Everyone nodded and vocalized their agreement as we affirmed our particular brand of activism and it's superiority to that of the crusty old-school white supremacists like the guys we were on the way to meet.

Dave Mentsoyan, the leader of DASH (the Detroit Area Skinheads), called them the "SS Acid Group" in sarcastic homage to their affinity for LSD. Dave was only able to tell us this and other things after a lengthy explanation of his Armenian heritage and corresponding swarthy skin-color. We were still wary of keeping company with someone who would look so at home wearing a turban, but gradually warmed up to him after witnessing his valor in the coming confrontation and hearing other respected skinheads vouch on his behalf. Dave also claimed that his grandfather had personally rounded up Jews while serving in an Armenian SS group during WWII, so if Armenians were good enough for Hitler I guess they were good enough for us.

Our opinion of Ken Dunn and his SS Action Group headed in the other direction, and faster as we spent more time with them.

Arriving at Dunn's ramshackle house in the Western Suburbs, we were greeted by one of his toadies who was dressed in a full-blown SS uniform. He was the type of dork who I shook down for lunch money every day in high school, emboldened by our presence and his swastika armband. Pat and I looked at each other and exchanged smirks and eye-rolls as we returned the salute given by the loser who would more likely have been smashed by the real SS rather than recruited. We followed him into the house, where we met all 6 of the other SS Action Group members, all of them in full regalia. Ken Dunn himself rose to welcome us wearing the meticulously pressed and adorned uniform of a high-ranking SS officer, which produced a kind of gay S&M effect when teamed with his neatly trimmed beard and ponytail. My first thought upon seeing him was that if he dared to display a condescending bent-arm salute, the kind reserved for only Hitler and his inner circle, I was going to knock him the fuck out and lead my boys in a vicious stomp of his unconscious body. But Dunn knew better, this day not being his first picnic with skinheads, and shot up his right arm in a crisp, full salute which we again returned.

"Hail Hitler my *white brothers!* Thank you for traveling

to *join our struggle!* You men look like you can *handle yourselves.* Are you ready to *smash some reds?*" He spoke with an uncomfortable quasi-monotone that wavered towards the end of each sentence.

A small dusty TV looped a VHS copy of *Triumph of the Will* in the living room behind him. I got the feeling that Ken and the other 6 members of the Fourth Reich spent the bulk of their leisure wearing out Leni Riefenstahl's work of Hitlerama while spun out of their gourds on robust biker acid. Dunn had the fucked-up demeanor of a life-long loser with zero public-speaking ability who nonetheless spent hours in front of a bathroom mirror desperately trying to channel the intense manner of Adolph Hitler. His dwindling handful of followers remained so only because they were somehow lamer than him.

"Reds and anyone else who wants some." I casually replied, noticing the hollowness behind Ken's shifty blue eyes. I saw a man who had nothing to offer the world. Someone who had failed time and again since a most likely shitty dysfunctional childhood and now, in his mid-life, had nothing but silly costumes and Hitler footage to cling to. Yet my brothers and sisters and I had travelled 8 hours to take part in his shindig. Why was that? Well, for starters, our DASH boys were the ones who invited us, and it was great to meet them in person after a series of post-office-box correspondence. And the idea of an epic brawl with Jews, communists, queers, and all manner of non-white filth was too tempting to pass up. Prior to that day, none of us had first-hand experience in an actual public white power rally. So there we were, reluctantly allowing ourselves to be led into battle by a pathetic long-haired druggie.

Pat was right beside me and also staring down Dunn. "You just show us where they are and we'll take care of shit Milwaukee-style." He said with an assured confidence.

"Excellent! That's what we *like to hear*! You'll see that aside from going to *different barbers*, the SS Action Group has much in common with *skinheads*; we both prefer *action over words!*" Dunn's eyes remained emotionless as his face pantomimed what I think was supposed to be a smile to match Pat's sincere one.

Ken Dunn made my skin crawl, and I could feel the remnants of my blood-alcohol unpleasantly metabolizing, so I left him to Pat and went to talk to Dave about the beer situation, which we got sorted in short order. About 5 of us made the trip to the beer store and back, bristling at the countless blacks and arabs we saw along the way. Every day was a rally when you were a skinhead. We didn't play dress-up one day a year and then fade back into mundane society when the dust settled. As much as Dunn liked to portray his motley bunch as akin to ours, we all knew that the bold brotherhood of skinheads heralded a new dawn for the white power movement. Not to mention we were simply that much cooler than everyone else.

A 26' U-Haul sat outside the house upon our return.

The rear door was open and the skinheads that were piling in raised a rousing cheer at the sight of the beer we carried. As we were loading the cases of Milwaukee's Best, the SS Acid Group was raising a cache of what looked like shields from Ken's basement. Upon closer inspection, they were indeed shields, fashioned from stolen stop-signs spray-painted black, with neatly duct-taped swastikas on the business side and handles made from bits of garden hose bolted on the other. I grabbed one and hefted it. It felt good. Doing my best to conceal a glimmer of respect for the SS Action Dorks, I said to Ken, "These are pretty cool. What do we need them for?"

Then noticing the motorcycle helmets he and his bunch toted, I deduced the answer before he replied, "Oh, you'll be glad to have those! The reds will be assaulting us from afar with rocks and bricks and *whatever else they can dig up!* They are cowards who are terrified to engage in close combat with *Aryan Warriors!* Teddy will also be around to *hand out the batteries.*"

"Batteries?!"

"Yes sir! We of The SS Action Group save our dead batteries all year long *for this occasion!* You can *throw them at the reds!*"

"Heh! Right on. I'll take a bunch."

With flight jacket pockets full of corroded C and D cells, I climbed up into the U-Haul to settle in sitting on my shield with a beer in each hand. Over the course of the hour ride to Ann Arbor, we inhaled beer while trading glorious war stories. Dave's boys proudly told of his signature move, "The Mentsoyan Stomp", which involved jumping off the hood, sometimes roof, of a parked car to land boots on a downed opponent's head. Dave himself just smiled sheepishly in response. I made a mental note to try that technique myself the next time an opportunity arose. Not to be outdone, Pat skalded the tale of our recent hippie house boot party, elaborating on my juggernaut performance after being clocked with a lead pipe. Illustrating the story with my still-healing scar to prove it, I was interrupted by Tina, who quipped, ". . .let me guess, then you pissed on him?"

The excited drunken laugh shared by the lot of us was rudely interrupted by a deafening THUNK that shook the truck. We felt the truck slow down and were shaken by more thunderous banging from outside, in increasingly rapid succession. It sounded like it was raining bowling balls. Pat and I gave each other a pre-fight check-in glance and looked around to our crew to make sure everyone was ready. The small window to the cab slid open to reveal Ken's helmeted mug. "Welcome to Ann Arbor comrades!" He beamed, this time sounding quite authentic.

The muffled roar of a huge angry crowd accompanied the booming impact of whatever heavy objects were barraging the U-Haul, a roar that rose to suck up all other sounds as the rear door was slid open to reveal a double-line of riot cops between us and a seething rainbow mob that clamored for our blood. Ken had a bullhorn in one hand and his shield in the other. "ARYAN WARRIORS: *MOVE OUT!*" he droned through it, as we poured out of the truck and proceeded in the only direction available—a narrow causeway between walls of police that led in front of a huge glass-walled Federal building. Glass-walled?! Did the cops under-estimate the protesters?

Pat and I each got to either side of our Milwaukee crew and raised our shields to protect them as well as ourselves, even though they had shields of their own, as we hustled to the designated spot; a smallish raised area better suited to guitar players with slowly but steadily growing piles of coin and small bills gracing their open guitar cases than a besieged lot of skinheads and dipshits in SS get-ups.

We ultimately formed a line in front of a banner held up by the SS Acid guys that said WHITE REVOLUTION IS THE ONLY SOLUTION along with their P.O. Box. The banner was canvas, and stretched tight enough to bounce the hail of rocks that hit it to land on our backs. The relentless assault of bricks and rocks coming from the front was much more of a concern though. I hopped as a chunk of asphalt beaned my knee. They were literally tearing up the fucking sidewalk and throwing it at us!

I peeked to either side of my shield, looking for a target to sidearm an Energizer at. The mass of protesters stretched as far as I could see, at least in the quick glimpses I dared to take. They carried banners of their own, saying things like DIE NAZI SCUM! and NEVER AGAIN! along with rainbow flags and of course red ones with hammers and black fists and things about WORKERS written on them. Best of all were the numerous peace signs that prevailed amongst the bloodthirsty black, white, yellow, and brown mob. A white guy about my age with stringy whipping blonde dreadlocks and a tie-dyed Grateful Dead shirt was screaming so hard it looked like he was about to have an aneurysm. Just as he fired a sidewalk-chunk that narrowly missed Jane, smashing into the glass building behind us, I zeroed-in on him and whipped a battery that flew wildly off-target to land somewhere deep in the crowd.

Dunn paced back and forth between us and the banner, yelling though the bullhorn about race-mixers and Jews. That inflection at the end of his phrases remained throughout, amplified and distorted and even more irritating. "WHITE PEOPLE OF *ANN ARBOR*: THIS IS THE *SS ACTION GROUP!* WE ARE HERE TO EXPOSE THE JEWISH CONSPIRACY *AGAINST OUR PEOPLE!* YOU CAN JOIN WITH US OR BE CRUSHED BY THE COMING *WHITE REVOLUTION!!*"

The mob became somehow even more enraged as Dunn rambled on, surging against the police line. There's no doubt in my mind they would have torn us limb-from-limb if given the chance. The SS Acid Batteries we brought began to fly back at us, as we gathered stones and cement from the ground and recycled likewise. The sound of shattering glass highlighted the din of the confrontation as more and more of the windows behind us became casualties. More than a few of our shaved heads were marked with blood from flying broken glass, batteries, rocks, bricks, you name it, as were the faces of our adversaries. I was beginning to wonder how much longer the cops could hold the commies back when they began to corral us back towards the U-Haul.

I was exhilarated! The drunken self-destructive part of me was itching to go wading into the crowd of blacks and Jews with my shield and a D-cell fortified fist despite the overwhelming odds, but considering that we had Jane and Tina and a bunch of other girls with us, not to mention the desperate pleading of the elusive self-preservation part of me, I helped clear a path for withdrawal instead.

Our escape route was rapidly collapsing as the peace-loving protesters clawed their way past the cops. A Jewish-looking man slipped through and took a swing at one of the SS Acid guys. Dave jumped between them and swung his shield to catch the Jew in the mouth with the edge of it, knocking a bunch of his teeth out. He turned to put himself between us and the mob. Pat and I joined him, alternately throwing punches and rocks and we backed into the truck. The three of us were the last ones in, jumping up as it pulled away. Something heavy skipped off my head and I kicked back at hands grabbing for my boots as my crew hoisted me to safety.

The truck accelerated and we hung out the back, saying goodbye to our new friends with defiant salutes as the last rocks sent us off.

After we shut the door and got underway, I cracked a beer and gave myself a going-over to assess damage. I had a mean knot on my right knee and another on the back of my head, along with a bunch of small cuts in various stages of bleeding. Nothing serious, especially considering the hundred-to-one odds. Everyone was busy telling their version of the melee in frantic but relieved voices. I was slamming beers as usual, but unusually quiet as I contemplated the hypocrisy I had just witnessed.

Holy shit did those people hate us! So much for free speech. These motherfuckers were screaming for our blood while waving rainbows and peace signs in the air! Peace and love as long as you behave. As long as you conform and accept the multi-racial dogma. If you dare to think for yourself and stand up for your folk then they'll peace and love you all the way to a prison cell, or a grave. Anyone with the audacity to question the status quo was portrayed as a monster. We enraged them because we had the guts to stand up. To fight back. It made me think that everything I was reading about race and the Jews was spot-on.

During the 6 months leading up to that day, I had devoured an intense regimen of streetfighting, studying racial ideology, and obscene alcohol consumption. It was almost eerie how the further down that road I went, the more society would seem to vindicate my burgeoning racial awareness.

I felt an ominous sense of my coming role in this struggle.

arno michaelis

6: Martyr's Day

Facing a massive bonfire, I stood with my arm raised in a crisp Nazi salute. My crew of Northern Hammer Skinheads and our Confederate Hammer comrades mirrored the salute as we formed a ring around the fire.

The date was December 8th, 1988. We were celebrating Martyr's Day in a forest about 50 miles outside of Tulsa, Oklahoma. I watched the stout muscular silhouette of Jim Denko pace around the fire as he spoke with a determined fury about the man we came to pay tribute to.

In 1983 Robert J. Matthews founded the Brüder Schweigen, or "Silent Brotherhood"; a small cadre of hardened men also known as "The Order", who declared war against the United Sates government in the name of the white race.

The roaring flames of the bonfire reflected in our eyes as we stood sweltering in its heat that drove back the cold damp night. Denko gestured in a grandiose arc as he described the men of The Order gathered around one of their infant daughters, raising their arms as we were as they swore an oath to protect her and all white children from the horrors of the mud races.

A year before this night I was just a hooligan, in it for the drinking and fighting. That night a surrogate of Robert Matthews burned a searing love for my race into my soul, amplifying the torrid romance with exponential violence. I spun recollections of the senseless brawls and beatings that bloodstained my hands, until they became glorious acts of heroism. Just like the Brüder Schweigen, I was a valiant warrior defending my race against the Jews, who tirelessly sought to bury my people under a stinking tide of mud-races. I convinced myself that I cared about that symbolic white baby, in order to fuel my thirst for violence.

As Denko passionately elaborated on the Jewish plan for our genocide, my brow furrowed and nostrils flared. Adrenaline surged through my body at the thought of tearing the Jews and niggers limb from limb with my bare hands. Hearing of Robert Matthews being burned alive by federal agents, each of his charred hands still on the triggers of assault rifles, evoked an overwhelming need to avenge him and ultimately join him in Valhalla after dying in battle myself.

With a resounding climatic vigor, Jim Denko spoke the Fourteen Words;

"We must secure the existence of our people, and a future for white children!"

50 of us repeated in a single thundering voice, then spontaneously answered, "HAIL ROBERT MATTHEWS! HAIL THE ORDER!" as our salutes raised up and down in perfect unison.

When the day comes, we will not ask whether you swung to the right or whether you swung to the left; we will simply swing you by the neck.

7: hall· fire· razor

The Hall was a complex of buildings on the corner of 4th Street and Greenfield Avenue on Milwaukee's predominately Hispanic Near-South Side.

I was in an efficiency in the corner-most building, behind that was a cottage that Will Thompson and his girl Dena were renting, and just to the north of them, on Greenfield, was another cottage where Matt Thompson and Brett lived. Since the moment we moved in, there was a collective housewarming party that revolved from host to host and seemed to remain in full effect indefinitely.

After a particularly sloshed Friday night, I was awakened by a call from Will; "Arno: you better get up! That house next door to you is on fire—your fuckin' place is gonna burn down!"

Still in a stupor, I slammed the phone down and wrote it off as Will thinking he was cute waking me up at the ungodly hour of 9:00 am on a Saturday. I was fading back into inebriated slumber when my door shook with a frantic pounding. Stumbling out of the rummage-sale sleeper-sofa I called a bed, I noticed ravenous leaping flames immediately outside my back window. Will, Matt, and Brett piled in as I opened the door and started grabbing my few things worth saving, which consisted of a battered TV and a few milk-crates full of clothes and

Dungeons & Dragons books. I was already carrying my shotgun, which I slept with anyway, and after snatching-up the army surplus ammo box full of slugs and 00 buckshot shells, I chased after the guys back to Matt and Brett's to complete the evacuation.

Firefighters were already on the scene, hammering the blaze with a battery of turgid hoses. Beams of pressurized water transfixed the house next-door to mine, while the raging fire angrily fought back from within. Glass rained down as the rear upper window exploded to release boiling steam byproduct of the tangling flame and fluid. As the firefighters pelted the burning house from every angle, stray streams smashed the 2nd story window in Will's house, sending water by the hundreds of gallons to flood it. Fortunately, the bulk of their stuff had been cleared from the house already. We scrambled in for a final sweep of valuables before the place was completely waterlogged. Still being wasted from the night before turned the hurried emergency chore into an adventure.

We had been on a rockabilly kick for the past few weeks, so Brett had a Jerry Lee Lewis tape handy and blasting *Great Balls of Fire* seemed to be the natural choice of a soundtrack. We all sang along, laughing as we settled on to Brett and Matt's back porch to crack the few remaining beers and enjoy the spectacle.

The displaced occupants of the burning house weren't as amused by our choice of music as we were. They were a black family, consisting of maybe 2 or 3 sisters and some ridiculous amount of kids between them. We were firmly convinced that they were a group of welfare warriors commuting between Milwaukee and Chicago for the better Wisconsin benefits.

The truth of our bigoted assumption was never fully established, but they never seemed to go to work and there was a consistent amount of turnover, so there were observations to support the theory. They all got out safely, but they weren't as fortunate as we were to have rescued their belongings. There was much shrieking and carrying-on over lost possessions, and we didn't make the slightest effort to conceal our amusement at their plight, responding to their angry shouts with gleeful raised fingers and beers. A fresh chorus of cackles erupted each time Brett rewound the tape to keep *Great Balls of Fire* looping in accompaniment.

The enormous black women were easily mad enough to attack us, and I was pondering how to react to that when the white-trash landlady we had dubbed "The Land-Hag" came rolling up in her jacked-up F150.

She was this hideously ugly woman from somewhere up north where we all assumed there was some sort of trailer complex she originated from. Brett would specifically point out every time she was mentioned that the fat of her gut hung down and had this kind of double-chinned pussy effect. It was particularly obvious and all the more-so disgusting and accentuated by the fact that she was partial to stuffing herself into very tight jeans. To top it off, she was very homely, had a horrible complexion, her breath stank, her teeth were yellow, and she had this stringy rat-hair along with a personality abrasive enough to strip paint. She was foolish enough to rent to us, so I guess we did appreciate that, but otherwise she was a typical slumlord who wouldn't have fixed any of the myriad hazards on her properties even if any of us were ever sober enough to notice them.

Immediately upon the Land-Hag's arrival, the ire of the Welfare Warriors turned from us to her. Heated accusations of arson flew, and before the Land-Hag could even plead her innocence, the punches flew as well.

Within moments there was this big raucous ghetto-black-welfare-family on up-north-white-trash-family catfight all over the sidewalk while the fire blazed on full bore. The firemen scrambled to keep the whole block from going up like a pile of barrio matchsticks and were successful in containing the original fire if not extinguishing it. One of them narrowly avoided being incinerated as the ladder he was on melted. He had to be snapped-up by a guy in a cherry-picker seconds before the ladder fell into the flames. With the firefighters thus engaged and ourselves busily drinking and heckling there was no one to intercede in the Welfare Warrior vs. White Trash melee.

The Land-Hag and her daughter, who was just as ugly, but as scrawny as her mother was bulbous, were pretty much at the mercy of the large and actually pretty intimidating Welfare Warrior matriarchs. According to standard racist protocol we would have been behooved to jump-in on behalf of the white women, but considering our personal distaste for them and the unspoken but mutually acknowledged unwillingness to brawl a bunch of colossal black females, we chose instead to egg the fight on, shouting encouragement to combatants from both camps.

Land-Hag and daughter had been getting their asses whooped up and down the sidewalk for a good few minutes or so, when one of the black ladies ripped out a sizable chunk of ratty dirty-ass Land-Hag hair and waved it about wildly to accentuate the flying curses and charges of arson. We raised a cheer for the partial scalping as if it were a Superbowl-winning touchdown just as the police arrived and set about their perpetual task of fun-ruining. The Welfare Warriors dispersed in bittersweet homeless victory and the Hags fled the scene spitting gravel and smoking debris from 4x4 treads.

It took the firefighters the rest of the day to get the fire under control, and by the time they did, Will's cottage was utterly swamped. My building was quite soggy on the outside, but otherwise unscathed. The unoccupied apartment upstairs was the logical place for Will and Dena to go, while the entire double-digit roster of the Welfare Warriors piled into the 1-bedroom a thin wall away from my efficiency.

The entire place was a rundown roach motel. Everything was broke, everything was old. In my bathroom there was a fucked-up light fixture clawing its way out of the yellowed drop-ceiling. Showers of sparks celebrated my arrival every time the light switch was thrown. During rare moments of sobriety I would make mental notes to either leave the bathroom light on or not turn it on in the first place. Then I would promptly submerge those and any other life-preserving notions in an ocean of beer until the sparks flew once again. The glaring fire hazard was but a tree in the forest of threats to my life that I ignored if not embraced, daring fate to come for me, perhaps in subconscious acknowledgement of the wrong I had become. I was one drunken piss away from immolation.

The lot of the Welfare Warriors stuffed into the rooms adjacent to mine made for quite a ruckus. If I would have been a normal hardworking guy who went to sleep at a reasonable time instead of when the beer ran out, I would have been pretty aggravated by the noise.

But as it was they were doing us a favor by serving as a living exhibit to prove whatever racist point that we were trying to make. Any time that someone would say that we were stretching truths or making unfair accusations about the living conditions of your typical black person, we would point to our kindly neighbors and the 20 of them living in a one bedroom apartment as if they were completely able to improve their situation but too lazy and stupid to do so.

We used them as a device to justify our ideology; not only while proselytizing but also during the constant internal reinforcement that racism requires. If you're going on a premise that the white race is something special and that it needs to be saved from "non-whites", you need to be able to justify the hows and whys of that —namely the whys. Why your people are superior to their people. Never mind that your way of life is almost indistinguishable from theirs. Never mind that you're a raging alcoholic and that you work a shitty minimum-wage job and that you go around and start fights with honest people on the street. That's all really beside the point, because you are "fighting for your race", and your race is something worth saving because pretty much anything worth anything was, according to us, invented by white people. We made a point to overlook any contributions to culture or technology made by ancient Arabic, American, Asian, and especially African people. In our own twisted way we associated any of their accomplishments with that of our own people. They had stolen white technology. All they had was leeched from the white man's unique ability and creativity. When you're thinking that way, it comes in really handy to have someone right next door to you who seems to exemplify everything bad that you seek to stereotypically saddle upon the enemy, and the Welfare Warriors certainly suited that role.

Their tenure at the apartment next door didn't last long, as the Land-Hag soon produced a legal means to evict them along with sheriffs to see it through. Once they were gone, we completed our take-over of the remaining buildings on the corner.

Exploring the place, we found that the attic was actually pretty cool. We cleaned a bunch of junk out of it, exposing the beams, which were actual old-style 2" by 4" 2x4s, joists, and roof-boards. The aged lumber framed a natural setting for us to create "The Hall", in tribute to the Viking long-hall.

Our first priority was to construct a bar, which we built with wood scrapped from the smoldering and/or flooded ruins adjacent to us. We adorned the vaulted attic roof with ill-begotten flags of all the white countries of the world—symbols of our impending conquest. Below each flag hung our individual shields, lovingly crafted and painted with bold swastikas, sunwheels, and other symbols of our folk. A collection was taken to purchase enough cheap folding chairs to seat about 50, which were deployed for weekend meetings and stowed erstwhile in favor of heavy-bags that we diligently beat the hell out of between actual streetfights. The melange of sweat, smoke, alcohol, and blood dry-roasted into a potent waft that accentuated the prevailing sense of Racial Holy War that we sought to promote.

Our disparate members from Racine and Kenosha were up every weekend, if not every night of the week. Booze-soaked conversation looped in regards to how we're going to save the white race and why whites were so much better than everyone else. Our individual failures by prevailing societal standards to make money and consume things other than beer were buried under majestic tales of our collective racial greatness.

A focused soundtrack of white power rock-n-roll inspired our bond to each other and crucial hatred for everyone else. Brutal Attack, a seasoned oi! band from Britain, had just released their 3rd album, *Tales of Glory*, whose title-track quickly became the theme-song of The Hall. Night after night was spent immersed in our own Tales of Glory.

The few years of involvement that myself and the other senior members of our crew had survived were rife with gory true-stories of wanton violence; the hippie-house lead pipe incident, the Skin-fest of '88 and all the beatings that went down that summer, the Downer street riots, and the bravery of Pat O'Malley on Amy Place when he shot a kid attempting a drive-by on our house—all of the particularly violent, and as we viewed them, glorious moments leading up to that time.

The steady stream of new recruits driven to us by integrated schools and street crime were force-fed copious amounts of cheap beer until the Tales of Glory evoked a primal vibe of vengeance and righteousness. They would listen with bloodshot starry-eyes as we told about all the great times we had randomly beating people who didn't deserve it, then mentally superimpose the palpable punt of past boot-parties upon the black guys who beat them up after school or mugged them in an alley.

Our yarns were spun into a kind of mythology that not only justified our positions as leaders of our pack, but also served to set a watermark of the level of dedication we expected of nascent race warriors.

It was a "by all means necessary" approach. We were at war with non-whites. We were at war with complacent white race-traitors who failed to recognize the gravity of our mission. Because we were at war, there was no such thing as a fair fight. When you are at war, you must make a point of not having fair fights. If you are at war and you find yourself getting in fair fights, you are fucking up. For that reason we felt that any sort of beating was justified. If there were 10 of us and one sorry black guy who was at the wrong place at the wrong time, he was going to feel the boots of 10 guys on him.

That kind of violence perpetuated itself, and regularly brought about situations where we were outnumbered ourselves. From the standpoint of being warriors, we embraced those outnumbered situations and gauged our worth according to our performance against fearsome odds. That was really what split the men from the boys; it was real easy to jump in and be a part of a 10 on 1 in your favor beating, but when it was an entire bar full of people armed with baseball bats and pool-sticks against you and a few of your brothers, you gained a whole new perspective about what it means to be in a streetfight.

We instilled that perspective on impressionable young kids who were emotionally scarred at tender ages by shitty home lives, racial violence, alcoholism, and whatever other dysfunction du jour that moved them to seek us out.

The Hall soon became a violence machine, churning out conscience and empathy-free menaces that roamed Milwaukee assaulting innocent people in the name of a Racial Holy War we had fabricated for them. The street violence that began during the 700 Club days travelled a dramatic upward spike that culminated at The Hall; to the point where the sheer ferocity came to concern we who had initiated it.

It was also at The Hall where the allegiance and nature of our group started to shift from a skinhead crew to that of a more cerebral racial organization. The preceding summer, Will and I had been down to the Church of the Creator (COTC) headquarters in Otto, North Carolina, where we spent 2 weeks studying the ideology of Creativity and paramilitary survivalism.

The COTC was as violent and ruthless as any racial group there was, promoting a vehemently anti-Christian, pro-white agenda that advocated genocide against all non-whites and white race-traitors along the way to a "Whiter and Brighter World". But it was also much more pragmatic. The far-sighted and comprehensive approach to white victory that the COTC espoused stated that winning the hearts and minds of our fellow whites should be our priority at the time, not simple street hooliganism, which is really all that skinhead action had amounted to.

We loved to drink ourselves into oblivion. We loved to get in fights. We loved to get hit and we loved to hit things. In order to have any kind of longevity in such an environment, you have to have those qualities. The people who were afraid of violence—the people who we felt were cowards—would ultimately be weeded out. The first thing that happens to someone who is obviously not geared for such combat is that they are ridiculed and ostracized from the group. If they don't grow a pair and start instigating violence themselves—if they don't start creating their own Tales of Glory—the ostracization continues and ultimately winds up with the person in question getting the shit kicked out of them by their own crew. This would happen quite often.

That's the kind of mindset that we had begun our racial activism with. Our experience up until then was based around that ultra-violent, survival-of-the-fittest, kill-or-be-killed philosophy. It was really just a desperate extension of teen angst lashing-out at the world. COTC ideology was just as desperate and explicitly based on the same core belief of might-makes-right, but much more calculated in regards to the means to the end. It occurred to us that our status quo of drunken street-fighting was not really doing anything to further our goal, which was the preservation of the white race. As our ideology became more advanced, as the knowledge-base behind our beliefs grew, it became apparent that we had to change the way we were doing things.

Thus we found ourselves in an ironic position; we would draw those kids to us because we were storied street-brawlers, yet we were evolving to discover that the street-brawling was ultimately counterproductive. The

Tales of Glory gained a preface that read like, "Yeah, this is how we used to do it. It was great. It was a lot of fun to go out chasing black people around for the hell of it, BUT, don't you go doing that. What you need to do is get good grades and go to college and get a good education and a good job so you can be a person of influence in the community" ...a person of influence in this society that we had declared war upon. Ultimately people with money and power who could really affect changes toward the end that we were looking for.

We began thinking more along the lines of the big picture, where members of our group would move beyond the destitute poverty that we were all living in, but not for personal gain—strictly to gain capability for the movement.

Ben Klassen was the leader of the Church of the Creator. He was a crusty old codger, and not very impressive in person, but nonetheless a capable writer and racial philosopher. The books of Creativity that he wrote and the organization behind them were all things that happened because he was a fairly wealthy self-made guy. For many of us he was the first rich guy we ever met and talked to in our lives. Meeting someone with means beyond a ghetto apartment and beer money for the evening, and seeing the impact that they could have as far as advancing the racial movement was concerned, impressed upon us the need for a change in direction.

True to form, we had a debatable degree of success practicing what we preached. We still all drank profusely.

We still found ourselves getting in fights all the time. That kind of lifestyle is extremely difficult to just switch off. But we did make a solid effort and results slowly began to manifest.

We had the best of both worlds at our peak in the sense that we were looked upon as a physical force on the streets by the youth who we were most interested in; yet at the same time, as we obtained more sophisticated literature to pass out and as we became more well-versed and well-spoken in the propaganda ourselves, we were also able to increase our contact outside that typical target group and more into mainstream white society, which is ultimately where we wanted to be.

We tried to concentrate on refining our message and increasing our level of sophistication, which involved a lot of "do as I say and not as I did" instruction to the younger guys. The bulk of our crew had enough respect for (and fear of) us to take the new direction to heart, but there were always the fringe-of-the-fringe guys who posed as much of a threat to our organization as they did to the rest of the world.

There were two in particular who were hellbent on making their own Tales of Glory the goriest of all: Floyd Russel and Timothy "Big Mac" McClellan.

Just as it was for me at the beginning, race was simply a convenient excuse to brutalize people as far as they were concerned. Disturbed, outcast kids who had a ton of hate and hurt within them. They were prime candidates for us to wind-up and set loose on an unsuspecting society. And that's exactly what we had done. As Will and I and a lot of the older guys from Racine and Kenosha grew into a more intellectual exercise of our racist beliefs, these guys were still fully engaged with the idea of going on manhunts and piling into some hunk-of-shit beater car at every opportunity to find someone to assault.

We decided to stop being hooligans ourselves and hope that they caught on. But as we made it plain that there was to be no more mindless violence, they went out on their own to pick up where we left off. As we would gather in The Hall and simmer schemes to get our message to Joe Six-Pack White Guy in the most effective way possible, Floyd and Mac would be out on the town taking the notion of fucking people up to new levels.

As the effects of daily street violence wore off, terrifying questions squirmed from my indomitable human core—a part of me that had been suppressed for years. Were we fighting now so we could kill later? Kill people by the billions? What would really happen when the Whiter and Brighter World came to fruition? Would we—would I—truly have the stomach to pull the trigger on a genocidal scale?

I tried to focus on the facts as I had known them; that *they* were not people, that it was *them* or us, that the future of our children was at stake. Considering the grave circumstances, what choice was there but to fight back by any means necessary? Everywhere we turned in our world, we saw nothing but the insidious workings of the enemy. It was a matter of the most righteous self-defense possible to win at any cost and eliminate any possibility of future threats by wiping every last non-white and race-traitor off the face of the Earth.

That's how we sold the curbing of senseless drunken beatings to our crew, and to ourselves. Neither pitch was entirely successful. The welcome blossom of thought and consciousness first sprouted during those times, even though I wouldn't realize it until I began the self-discovery of writing over a decade later. There was also a palpable wet blanket of exhaustion that weighed upon us elder members. Impending lofty epiphanies or not, we were all simply burning out.

A healthy bunch of our proteges however, were just getting warmed up. Floyd had just read Anthony Burgess' *A Clockwork Orange*. The Kubrick film had long been a favorite of skinheads, with those of us smart enough to catch the profound social message of the story making sure to bury it in appreciation for a bit the old ultraviolence. Awash in a culture of ultraviolence, doggedly believing in the honor of combat and the future glory of Valhalla, the brutality of both the book and the film was seen as the height of entertainment.

In the novel, the preferred weapon of the anti-heroic Alex was a straight razor, and before he even finished reading it, Floyd had taken to carrying one himself.

"Dude! It was only like five bucks at Walgreens! I been sharpening the shit outta it!"

For a couple of weeks he was walking around with this

thing and just itching to carve someone up with it. There were a number of incidents where the straight razor got pulled out and waved around. Fortunately for whoever they were fucking with that night the intended victim got away un-straight-razored for one reason or another.

All of this happened when they were off on their own, as we had made our lack of amusement with the straight razor quite plain. Will and I clearly saw a future where Floyd faced a felony charge and turned state's evidence on us to deal with it.

After weeks of scolding and appealing to a sputtering sense of higher calling, the only progress Will and I had made was to drive Mac, Floyd, and co. farther away from us and closer to running their own mutinous crew. Not that we missed them; we had plenty of more intelligent and thus more valuable comrades to preach to. But we were always concerned about what they knew of our own host of felonious acts that we had gotten away with.

We hadn't seen any of them in The Hall for an unusually long stretch of a week or so when Mac and Floyd came stampeding up the stairs in a hysterically cackling haze of boots and beer, bringing the Skrewdriver anthem Streetfight along with them:

"... but the skinheads have their own WHITE POWER!"

Will, Matt, Brett, and I had plenty of beers in us as well, but our evening had been spent practicing kickboxing on the heavybag and doling out bundles of Racial Loyalty newspapers for our latest distribution.

"Welly-welly-well! Good evening my droogies!" Floyd

slurred in piss-poor attempted Cockney.

Mac shuffled behind him huffing chuckles of "Heh! Heh!" in time with the hauling of his 275 pound bulk.

"Where the fuck have you guys been?! We got a shitload of RLs to put out. What did we tell you about priorities? And quit the Alex routine. It's painful." I said, rising from the bar.

Will looked up from his ale in irritation. "Are you here to help get the paper out?"

Stumbling for the bar, Floyd shot back, "Yeah, well, while you guys were folding newspapers, we were out on some REAL white power !"

We rolled our eyes as he continued, "Fuckin drivin down Wisconsin, we saw this nigger in a bus shelter, so we jumped out and tore the shit outta him! HAHAHAHAHA!!! Fuckin Mac hit him with this flying fuckin Black Belt Theater steel-toe, an then I fuckin took out me razor and got him all the way from like fuckin here (as he pointed at his temple) to fuckin HERE!!! (pointing to the tip of his chin) HAHAHAHAHA!!! Dude! Fuckin nigger blood EVERYWHERE! HAHAHA!!"

Mac's lager-reddened face lit up as he chimed-in. "Heh! Heh! Fuckin nigger was all 'AAHHH!!! AHHH! MAH FACE!' He was all tryin to hold his fucked-up nigger face together, all 'HEP ME! HEP ME!' Hehhehheh! Heh!"

"Yeah! And so I kept cuttin at him and Mac kept

bootin him! He had like 10 jackets on cause he was obviously a bum or whatever, so I dunno if I got to cut the motherfucker any more, but that one I got him was AWESOME! HAHAHA!!"

A couple of headbanger kids Mac recruited from the factory where he worked as a janitor tagged along behind them, so inebriated that I doubt they even knew what happened.

Mac lurched wildly for the fridge, "So where's the fuckin beers anyway?! Are you pussies coming out to manhunt some more with us or what the fuck?!"

Floyd was closest to me. I leaned in close to meet my booze-soaked eyes to his and said matter-of-factly, "We fuckin' told you no more manhunts. I'm gonna hit you now. Ready?"

After giving that second to soak in, I coiled then sprung my torso, whipping up my right elbow to wallop Floyd where his ear met his jaw. He collapsed in a limp heap for a few moments, then dragged himself to scale a distant chair, an imposing task under the combination of concussion and severe intoxication.

Doing something about it briefly crossed Mac's mind, until the Thompson brothers looked at him, at which time discretion became the better part of valor. Will stormed over to where Floyd lay draped over the chair like a bloody bar-rag.

"This ain't a game you assholes! This is the future of the WHITE RACE we're fighting for; and you're jeopardizing our whole fucking crew over some homeless nigger at a bus stop!! We're at war with the Jewish Occupational Government goddammit! What the fuck do you think you accomplished tonight aside from possibly getting us all busted—for nothing!! Did Robert Jay Matthews DIE so you could slash homeless niggers in bus stops?!" Will's open right hand flew up and bitch-slapped Mac across the face for punctuation.

Matt still sat at the bar. Lighting a cheap cigar and contemplating the flags on the walls, he said, "Get the fuck out of The Hall. Don't come back till you got your shit together. If we catch any heat from you dumb fucks you are both dead."

The lot of them slunk down the stairs sputtering almost inaudible curses. From the street there was a confused sequence of awkwardly ambulating boots and car doors slamming then the sound of bald tires squealing as they peeled out.

Brett watched them leave from the attic window. "Idiots. What the fuck are we gonna do with them?"

"Whatever. The more excuses I get to sock that dipshit, the better." It felt good to thunk an elbow on a person again after a couple-month hiatus. But it also felt bad to picture that guy holding his face together. Really fucking bad. I wrestled with the idea of saying so. A strained hush betrayed the possibility of the other guys thinking likewise.

Will was the first to bring us back to our hate. "Not like I give a shit about the nigger..."

8: epiphany

My daughter was conceived in acknowledgement to the shared belief of her mother and I that it was our duty as racially-conscious white people to produce white children.

A core tenet of white racialism is the fact that whites are being out-bred by "non-white" people at exponentially imposing odds. The idea that *there will be none of us left* is one that preys upon the already raging paranoia that prevails among racists and other fundamentalists. Once the fallacy that white people are a race unto themselves and a superior one to boot is bought into, it's not much of a stretch to link "the future of our race" to an uneducated, dysfunctional, alcoholic couple of 6 months planning a pregnancy they were by no means ready for mentally, emotionally, or economically.

Like fathers of every possible ethnic and socioeconomic background across the globe, I'll never forget the day my child was born.

Mom was a pro, ours being her 3rd daughter, and the labor portion was over after a relatively speedy couple of hours. Before I could get my bearings my kid was being whisked by a nurse from womb to a hamburger-warmer-looking contraption. Letting go of mother's hand, I rushed to meet my daughter face-to-face. She squirmed and did some obligatory crying, but her overall demeanor was much more relaxed than mine. Ours eyes met the moment she opened hers for the first time, and I felt a brief but timeless glimpse of the connection that would save my life over and over again.

But first mom would have that honor, a week after giving birth to her.

I wish I could say that looking into the magnificent blue eyes of my newborn daughter set me straight in an instant, but the truth is that I returned to my sophomoric drunken brawling within a matter if days.

My little brother and I had a case of beer down before we even headed out to the bar 6 days after I became a father-in-name-only. By 2am of the 7th day, we had thrown pitcher after pitcher of Sprecher and shot after shot of Cuervo in the mix, which of course behooved us to take a once-friendly game of pool with the locals outside for a full-blown donnybrook. Swerving away just far enough ahead of Port Washington's Finest to avoid apprehension, my brother and I cackled about our respective shiners and the amount of our opponents blood that had ended-up on my jacket as we sped home in his rusty old Bronco.

Bursting into the house with skinned knuckles and a proper testosterone buzz to go with the booze, my brother and I headed for the fridge to refresh our besieged memories as to whether or not there was any beer left.

Before we could find out, an extremely irritated new mother grabbed me by the arm and led me upstairs for a sound scolding. After a solid 30 minutes of expounding upon my worthlessness and utter failure as a father it was clear that there was nothing I could say in my defense. Rather than concede to the very valid and reasonable argument that I was a dad now and I shouldn't be out beating people up for kicks, I, in my inebriated wisdom, grabbed my EK combat dagger from the nightstand and challenged, *"is this what you want?!"* as I damn near took my left hand off with it.

That entire period of my life will remain forever hazed by the sick mist of alcohol, but the sensation of a snipped bass piano wire that sent a fountain of booze-laden blood firing from my wrist sears through that haze to this day. Screams of *"YOU FUCKING ASSHOLE!!"* accompanied by the crying of 3 little girls aged 4 years, 2 years, and 7 1/2 days faded to black along with the rest of the world.

Minutes later, I came-to long enough to take a swing at the paramedic who was desperately trying to replace the makeshift bedsheet bandage my girlfriend had fashioned in the process of saving my drunk ass from bleeding to death. Like all good skinhead girls, she was accustomed to the sight of blood, and well-versed in emergency first-aid.

Less and less frequent returns to semi-consciousness made appearances as my near-carcass was rushed to the emergency room. The audible chattering of my teeth and the taste of blood from my tongue that was bitten as a result were constant as an eternal coldness drew me away from light and motion.

By that time I had taken countless blows to the head with a wide assortment of blunt objects as a result of my streefighting habit. I had stared down the barrels of pistols, shotguns, and rifles and laughed even as bullets whizzed close enough to bring the hairs on the back of my neck to attention. In 1989, 3 years earlier, I had made a first drunken attempt at wrist-slitting with a broken Huber bottle after being told that I was 1/16th Native American by my mother. 2 years earlier my close friend Chuck was murdered in a post-bar brawl of his own. But none of those foolhardy moments gave me the slightest idea of what death was all about.

That sequence of images, sounds, and sensations between the snipping of my piano-wire tendons and the surgeon's anesthesia brought me as close to death as I had ever been. And somehow I managed to not learn a fucking thing from the experience.

Waking in the Intensive Care Unit 2 days later with one of my wickeder hangovers seasoned with the exquisite pain of severed nerves microscopically stitched together, the process of alternately being chastised and embraced by my girlfriend, my brother, my mom and dad, and the guys in my crew began. As it was in the moments prior to getting myself in that mess, I had nothing to say in my defense. Not that anyone was expecting behavior that was remotely logical from me at that point.

I spent a few days in the psychiatric ward per regulations for suicide attempt. After a brief evaluation by someone with a PhD after their name, it was concluded that "alcohol psychosis" and not plain old insanity had moved me to slash my left wrist to the bone with an 8" knife that was sharp enough for shaving.

I made a 30 day attempt at sobriety, the longest by far since I had commenced drinking at age 14. Sobriety that went out the window on my 22nd birthday when "...just one or two" Spaten Optimators were not only approved but encouraged by my girlfriend at the onset of the meticulously planned and successful surprise party she arranged for me.

Our relationship began an appropriately swerving, lazy but inevitably fatal nose-dive once the booze was back. My priorities remained drinking and fighting even as my severed wrist was slowly and painfully healing. I spent more time with my band Centurion, writing and performing vicious songs about how I was ready to kill and die for precious white babies, than I did spending time with the beautiful white baby of my own.

Her mother and I parted ways when my daughter was about 18 months old.

She moved to Key West where the father of her 2 older daughters was living, and made a half-assed attempt to take my daughter with her. It wasn't until faced with the prospect of being physically separated from my child that I realized my attachment to her. Having had such proximity to my death a year and a half earlier, all parties concerned had no doubt of the seriousness the vow of "over my dead body" I swore carried. With a few thousand dollars scraped together by my entire family, a custody agreement and the lawyer to make it stick was put into place.

I had become a single father at age 23.

1700 miles and dubious lifestyle choices came between my child and her mother. By the time my daughter was 3, even her maternal grandfather agreed that she was better off with her drunken father than her mother, who was busily engaged in the exploration of a new-found cocaine habit.

While this was going on, record-label drama with my band and the rapidly-increasing pace of our crew's self-destruction had deteriorated my faith in the white power movement. Following a trend among the more intelligent members of our organization, I began to spend much less time fretting over securing the existence of my race and a future for white children and much more time with my child.

Before I had fully shed my racist ideology, I called-off the race war with the realization that my daughter needed me. We were all each other had. Being a Racial Holy Warrior wasn't going to save my daughter; it would take me from her via death or prison. The more time I spent with her the more it became imperative that I leave the movement.

My band-mates, who were the last remnants of the skinhead crew that had been my family for the the past 7 years, all had families of their own in the works and were moved to cede to their exhaustion as I had.

As time passed I began to allow myself more and more contact with things that were once absolutely prohibited. Packer games. Seinfeld. Books about subjects other than race. By the time I welcomed back the Beastie Boys into my life, it was all over. However, the ability to enjoy hip-hop and TV sitcoms once again wasn't the true motivation behind my change of heart; that honor goes to my daughter.

By 1996 I was completely finished with the white power movement.

Traveling from one extreme to another, I sought out experiences that involved interaction with people I had once harbored a vicious hatred for. Blinded by bigotry, I had denied anyone who didn't share my skin tone the simple courtesy of conversation. Once that conversation was allowed to happen, I found that the fear that motivated me to hurt innocent people was utterly unfounded. People who I would have attacked on sight only a few years earlier regularly forgave me, accepted me, and embraced me.

As new friends took the place of old ones who were lost to death, prison, and the madness of racism, the positive energy involved inspired me to become continuously closer with my daughter. The pure beauty of her childhood is what ultimately demonstrated just how terribly wrong I had been.

There was one particular afternoon that drove the epiphany home:

I arrived early to pick my daughter up from daycare. No one had noticed me, so I took in the moment, watching with teared eyes as my little girl played with the other kids.

It struck me that the first thing I noticed was that they were all children; not black children, or white children, but the sons and daughters of mothers and fathers.

A young black man about my age walked in to pick up his daughter, who leaped into his arms and hugged him, the same way my little girl hugged me. The smile on his face as he listened to his child relate her day in a gleeful, excited stream was the same smile my daughter gave me on a daily basis.

I thought of all the people I had hurt, whether with my own hands or by lighting some psychopath's fuse. Those people had moms and dads and brothers and sisters. How did their loved ones feel when they saw this person who was so special to them battered and broken? How horrible would it be to have my daughter exposed to such violence in the slightest aspect?

Love for my child thawed a dormant empathy for humanity that I was never aware of.

9: raver

Paul had been telling me about rave parties all summer, trying to "recruit" me away from the limbo I was in and into the blissful spun-out rainbow family he had come to be a part of.

He kept talking about dancing, like it was this magical thing that took you away from all the world's ugliness— the ugliness that he and I had contributed to for so many years, and about the music that ". .transcended ego to reveal a universal oneness". On a less esoteric level, he also told me about the freely available and really good drugs along with the multitude of beautiful and friendly girls. This all sounded fantastic. So fantastic in fact that I just couldn't picture it. Dancing? I used to break-dance in my middle-school b-boy days, but since then the only dancing I had done was slam-dancing in mosh pits and a whole bunch of dancing on people's heads for no good reason. I couldn't picture myself dancing at the parties Paul described no matter how good the drugs were, and I didn't relish the idea of being the crusty old wallflower with the scars and swastika tattoos.

But Paul was the only friend I had at the time who I wanted to hang out with. The only guys from my old crew who I still talked to were my former band-mates, some of whom were still caught-up in race and all of whom were not very happy with me after I quit the band and later messed around with their new lead singer's girlfriend.

Paul lived in a flat almost on the UWM campus with a bunch of neo-hippie kids, some of whom actually went to college. While I still had an aversion to hippies, I found that after a healthy dose of marijuana and psilocybin mushrooms, neo-hippies were much nicer to hang out with than neo-nazis. As long as I could prevail on them to play the Beastie Boys and Led Zeppelin instead of the goddamn Grateful Dead. All the pot and psychedelics on Earth wouldn't have made that tedious crap any easier to stomach. So it was that I found myself over there every chance I'd get, learning the redeeming quality of a few good beers over the mass quantity of shit beer I had been accustomed to.

It was earlier that year that I had allowed myself to be reunited with the Beasties. I was all over them when License to Ill came out, but obviously had to set that aside along with the rest of my hip-hop past when I got caught-up in racism. I didn't really notice it happening. It was drink-fight-drink-fight-drink and the next thing I knew it was like I had never heard of The Beastie Boys.

Before he moved in with the hippies, Paul was staying at his dad's place in the notorious Meadows housing projects on Milwaukee's Northwest side. One afternoon Paul, Dave, and I were sprawled all over his room after breaking-in a ridiculously intricate bong we had built from Home Depot plumbing parts. Paul threw in *Check*

Your Head and from the first line of the first track, *Jimmy James*, I was rocked by the magnitude of my departure.

Well, people how you doing there's a new day dawning
For the Earth Mother it's a brand new morning

Indeed there was a new day dawning—again. Funny how it was Ian Stuart, lead of the primal skinhead band Skrewdriver, who struck me with title track of *Hail the New Dawn* almost a decade earlier. Hearing that song enticed me down a path rife with violence, hate, death, and imprisonment that I had narrowly escaped. Hearing this song was like a warm hug, letting me know that The Beasties forgave me even if I didn't forgive myself; that I was welcome back no matter where I had been.

By that time I had already lost my taste for saying the word "Jew" with venom, and for saying the word "nigger" entirely. But the irony of lying in a ghetto apartment, stoned out of my mind, listening to a bunch of Jews playing "nigger music" and marveling at how wonderful it felt was not lost on me. For the first time in my life, I thought about how the world was a much nicer place because of black people and Jewish people. And I thought about how one man's dawn was another man's nightmare.

Did I ever really believe in the "new dawn" of Skrewdriver and racist dogma? Now I wasn't so sure. I did daydream about what an "all-white" world would be like, back when the pursuit of such a twisted goal consumed me. But I never analyzed the idea in too much depth, because doing so exposed not just one, but a host of fatal flaws. Who decided who was "white" and who wasn't? Was Hitler-esque dictatorship the only way to govern, or was there such thing as "white democracy"? What happened to the billions of "non-whites" once the "Whiter and Brighter World" came about? Klassen and other racial thinkers had answers for all of that, but none of them really convinced me. I knew deep down that even in a racially homogenous society, people would find a reason to continue hating one another as long as the primal "might makes right" approach to life prevailed.

Up until an odd combination of strength and exhaustion aligned to lower my guard, "might makes right" was all I understood. As elementary as it may be, or as it should be to most human beings, the notion of people of all sorts not only living together peacefully, but thriving in cooperation was completely foreign to me. Until I was schooled by the Beastie Boys that is.

The three of us didn't say a word for the entire duration of the record, soaking in the delicious diverse harmony of the music. The farther away I was able to get from race, the better it felt. It was a weight not only off my shoulders but off my soul.

The sheer but very welcome strangeness of being around people who accepted me without a blood toll provided a sorely needed spiritual healing. I ached so badly to be away from my past, and Paul, who had already buried his skinhead demons, served as a beacon lighting the way to salvation.

But I was still skittish about the whole rave thing. Yeah, me, the big tough (ex)skinhead, veteran of battles and leader of troops was scared of dancing. As Paul got farther into the rave scene, there were more and more Saturdays when he was off at this party or that, leaving me to sit home drinking alone. I finally broke down on a Saturday afternoon in October of 1996 and asked him when and where the next party was. He answered "tonight" and "Chicago" and off we went.

Paul and as many raver kids that could fit in my dilapidated Ford Escort Pony (the entry level Escort) piled in and we headed for Chicago. "So any place in particular in Chicago?" I asked.

"We don't know yet." Paul replied.

"What?!" I wasn't comfortable with aimlessly wandering around Chicago. My skinhead instincts that equated big cities with dangerous other-than-white people and inevitable combat were still too fresh. I felt old and out of my element. And I didn't want to fight anymore.

Paul chuckled, "Chill out OG. We're going to the map point, where they'll give us directions to the party. It's a record store with an address even."

". . .and why can't we go straight to the party?"

"Cops. There tends to be less of them to deal with if the exact party location is kept under wraps up until the last minute. At least that's the idea. Not sure how effective the practice actually is, but it's kind of a tradition anyway."

Ah, a clandestine operation! That I could relate to. We made our way to the North side of Chicago and Gramaphone Records where a steady stream of kids in ridiculously huge pants was cycling through. Every single one of them looked so young and happy, like they had never been in a fight in their lives. Like they didn't know the meaning of the word "hate". I found myself strangely envious. Just a few years prior I would have been disgusted by them, and inclined to let them know by beating as many as I could catch into bloody pulps. That night though, all I wanted was to be as they were—pants and all! I looked down at my glaringly square high-wasted jeans that fit me and again felt an uncomfortable self-consciousness.

Paul noticed this and reassured me, "Don't sweat anything Arno. No one cares how you look or don't look or whatever. Just relax and have fun!"

I did my best to oblige him and tried not to reveal my continuing wonder as we ran in to get our tickets and directions. Apparently these parties all had names, this one being "Home." There was a long list of DJs on the directions flyer, none of whom I had ever heard of, but Paul and the rest of our group were busy chattering about them as we got back to the Pony.

"Paul Johnson is the SHIT!"

"Have you heard that Justin Long kid?"

"What, no jungle?"

"All house tonight! Duh."

"DOOD! Terry Mullan is at the afterparty!"

"Yeah, like he's gonna show up!"

They spoke the names of the DJs with an odd mix of reverence and familiarity, like these guys were simultaneously best friends and demigods. I was excited to experience the DJ mystique myself, but also fussing about the directions like an old man. As I got my Chicago bearings and realized where we were headed an involuntary alarm went off. "Holy shit Paul, you know this place is way on the South Side?!"

Paul rolled his eyes. "So?"

"So that's like the worst ghetto this side of fucking Detroit! We're seriously gonna spend a Saturday night there?!"

"And we're gonna love every minute of it. Quit being such a fucking pussy."

Paul knew me well enough to not only get away with questioning my courage but also to be able to use it to coax me along. I continued to drive and exercised every ounce of will I had to not lock the doors and freak out as we passed block after block of Chicago's severely depressed inner city. Still obsessed with strength and accustomed to spinning reality to suit my frame of mind, I decided that we were being not foolhardy, but carefree and strong as we penetrated the heart of the ghetto

The directions ultimately landed us in a huge vacant lot

that was rapidly filling with cars. The lot was behind a former roller-rink that was now in the long line of buildings awaiting a wrecking ball. A thick queue of party kids gathered length and breadth as it stretched from the battered back door of the building. Normally, the idea of standing in any kind of line didn't appeal to me, but I was almost fully bought-in to the rave idea at that point, and the people in line—most of them already dancing to the thump that radiated from the venue—had such an interesting, positive vibe about them that I didn't mind at all.

They were all so different! Not necessarily from each other, but drastically different from the day-to-day Joe and Jane Schmoes that you saw on the way to work, and seemingly from a completely different fucking planet than skinheads. I was so accustomed to uniform; not only uniform dress of shaven heads, boots and flight jackets, but also uniform skin color, mindset, and actions. I had been to many large gatherings of skinheads, where ridiculous amounts of beer was drunk, mean violent music was churned, and adrenaline surged as swastika flags were saluted and venomous speeches were made. We were not celebrating, but building massive walls around everything that made us the same, and preparing war against everyone and everything outside.

Without signs or speeches or symbolic flags, the common purpose of the rave kids was open, embracing, and nebulous all at once. And in a weirdly passive but irresistible way, so much more powerful than any fist, boot, blade or bullet could ever be.

Not one of the kids in line looked "white" to me. I'm sure many of them were ordinary white kids by day, but that night everyone lit up their own little star with unabashed personality in a race-free galaxy of color and warmth. Everyone displayed a unique incarnation of the same incredible style. They were all so effortlessly fucking cool but not giving a shit who was cool and who wasn't. Tiny creatures in massive clothes handmade from stuffed carnival animals and carpet remnants were gyrating with blinking-lights goggled alien-looking things amidst tall lithe runway bodies gleaming naked save for strategically placed electrical tape and glitter. Faery wings and devil horns. Brightly colored beads and baubles. Hi-lighted by shimmering rainbows, I noticed the beauty of an Asian eye. Of African lips. Of a Semitic nose. Traits that used to brand targets now smiled at me. With me. The realization that the two brightly-hued boys playfully kissing each other were breathing the same air as I was made my heart skip a beat. Then it occurred to me that they had beating hearts also. A simple biological fact that I would have vehemently denied a couple of years prior.

"Hey Wintage! You coming in or are you so ghetto fabulous that you want to stand around outside in it all night?" Paul was leading the rest of our bunch straight to the door, ignoring the line and its chromatic denizens. "Lines are for suckers."

I snapped out of my reverie and followed him to the entrance. A tall black guy with a Peterbilt baseball cap pulled down over his eyes and a face full of silver piercings gave a fond gold-toothed grin of recognition followed by a hug and a fistful of fluorescent pink paper wristbands to Paul, who handed them out to us and jumped through the wall of fog and lasers that designated the gateway to where we were going. I fumbled my wristband on and took a deep breath, feeling as much as smelling the stew of sweat, ghetto, smoke (fake, cigarette, and pot), eucalyptus, and electricity as I went through after him.

Lasers ran like fingers over my body as I stepped in. For a disorienting second I saw nothing but laser-lit fog, then I emerged into the vast oval that once circled with roller-boogied descendants of slaves, now literally thundering to the gigantic soulful bass of Chicago House music and packed butts-to-nuts with ravers, all of whom were moving wildly with the beat. A beat that rang forth not simply from the sound system or the DJ or the records he deftly wielded, but from the holistic tribal atmosphere that every attendee of the party helped to create. I shuffled agape into the dancing crowd, letting it envelope me, moving me through them and the music. A primal need to release myself, to release the grip of a lifetime of anger and hatred came over me. A lone obstacle stood in the way; I wasn't dancing.

Finding myself suddenly directly in front of the DJ, clothes and body cavities rocked by the humming whomp of low frequency sound, the dance issue was reflexively solved as the music physically shook me. I let go of my ego, setting aside thoughts of my past, what I was wearing, how I looked, and everything set in motion. Without consciously raising a foot or lifting a finger, I was swept up in the primal dance that has caressed humankind since we first walked upright. Timeless, relentless drums led the way to a sublime group consciousness. Blaring horns and synths accented samples of R&B vocal riffs that earnestly celebrated the rave mantra of peace, love, unity and respect. Time was marked only by the minute-hands of gleeful cheers that arose when the DJ would artfully change records, and hour-hands of the DJs themselves changing. Here and there, I would steal a glimpse away from my newfound inner self and out to the people around me.

To my left was one of the most beautiful women I had ever seen. She was tall, with the impossibly perfect bronze body of a comic-book super-heroine; only instead of tights and a cape, she wore pigtails and a neon-yellow bikini, the top straining to contain spectacular gravity-defying tits, the bottom peeking out above low-slung giant raver jeans that rode up and down her hips as they swung. Sweat glistened down her raised arms and exquisitely toned stomach, prismed by the sole light of the lasers and disco balls. Her eyes were closed and a look akin to genuine orgasm flushed her high cheekbones and full lips, which smiled to greet me as she noticed my attention. I could barely make out her voice even as she raised it to shout to me, "Hi! Are you having a good time?!"

"I'm having the best time of my entire life!" I shouted back.

"Awesome! I love this song!!" She replied. Then she blew my mind further by giving me a sweet kiss on the cheek before resuming her dancing. In the real world, I would have been frenzied into a caveman lust simply being in the presence of such a nymph, much less getting a kiss. In my old world, women were prizes won by measure of spilled blood. Sex was an animal gratification that happened in the dark, behind closed doors. That night on the South side of Chicago, mundane sexual urges were superseded by an all-encompassing common love and empathy that came as easy as breath. Rather than bristle and flex in an obsession to have her—like I automatically would have done in the past—I silently thanked the unnamed rave-goddess and returned to dancing myself, absolutely overjoyed that I had come out of my shell that night.

More tracks played. All of them with complimentary but distinct flavors. All of them bearing the same stitch of *BUmp-BUmp-BUmp-BUmp* four-four measure. There must have been a few thousand people in there if there was one, and that feeling of oneness kept amazing me over and over again as I danced. We were all cells in the same organism. I had experienced a very different oneness in the past. A singularity of hate and common enemies that I had a talent for focusing. This new oneness was so much better in every way. So much healthier. So much easier.

Opposite the Rave-Goddess, who was still dancing strong, I saw a couple of young men who were equally sweaty and scantily clad, locked in a passionate embrace that had no choice but to grunt and groove with the music. One had darker skin than the other, but my hardwiring that mandated immediate racial identification was long since in the process of failing, and being in the rave environment had completely short-circuited it, so I was happily surprised to notice not-noticing their precise race. I did notice that they were flamboyantly and unashamedly gay, and rather than vomit on the spot and commit a felonious assault, I smiled in knowledge that there were places like this—at least somewhere every Saturday night—where these guys could be themselves. When they became aware of me, I followed the Rave-Goddess lead and raised my voice to ask if they were having a good time.

"Fuck YES we are! Rock on brother!" was the response, followed by sincere hugs and high-fives, and the lot of us melted back into the sound.

Everyone experiences odd sensations now and then. But the feeling of my own sweat mingling with the sweat of flaming homosexuals and beautiful-beyond-beautiful women whilst vigorously shaking my ass to walloping House music in the wee hours of an Indian Summer Saturday night in the middle of the South side Chicago ghetto after having spent the past 7 years as a vicious white power skinhead was one for the Guinness Book of Odd. Oh, and I was sober as a judge, at least up until the point when a voice later identified as Paul's drew me from the dancefloor. "Look at this fuckin guy! Haha! Where the fuck have you been all night?"

"Oh shit! Has it been all night already? I hope not!"

"Naw, we got a while yet. Then there's the afterparty. Hey, come over to the chill room a minute, I got something for ya."

I was actually kind of irritated. I was enjoying myself as I never had before right where I was, but I followed along anyway to an even darker side room with slower, trippier music and a weirdly oozing floor that proved to be composed of writhing, intertwined, ecstasy-infused bodies. I was also enjoying yet another odd sensation of not being in charge for once. Paul held out his hand to hand me a pill. "Umm, yeah: dry the sweat off first dood."

I wiped my hands off on my sweated-through jeans, which didn't dry them much, and took a quick glance at the pill as I popped it. It looked like a baby aspirin but tasted like shit before I washed it down with an ice-cold bottle of water, also courtesy of Paul.

"You're gonna be feeling like about a million dollars in a little bit my man. Enjoy!"

"You're fucking awesome Paul."

"Holy shit, did you already eat some?!"

10: Charlie Dee's English 201

I took a second crack at an associate degree from Milwaukee Area Technical College in 1996, this time for "Computer Graphics and Multi-Media". It felt great to be taking classes and simply being in an academic environment. Going to school was the complementing daytime element of my integration back into a multi-cultural society. In class I interacted with people from all sorts of ethnic backgrounds for what seemed like the first time in forever. When you limit yourself to talking only to your own little Nazi cult for 7 years, then maneuver a complete 180 degree turn, it's like discovering the world all over again. For 7 years I hadn't sat down and had a conversation with anyone who wasn't white, and of whites, the only interaction I had with those outside of the movement was to proselytize them. The experience of learning together—be it about Adobe Photoshop, Economics, or Philosophy—with folks who I was very ashamed to admit a former irrational hatred for supplemented the healing process between Saturday night rave sessions.

My second semester in I wound up doing most of the teaching in my Photoshop class, having taught myself the software back in the t-shirt printing days. The act of facilitating another person's learning was incredible. As I went from workstation to workstation, I felt as much as saw people's beautiful individual souls as their respective light bulbs snapped on heralding the comprehension of a new bit of knowledge. Those light bulbs were all the same color. The shine of learning and accomplishment was a pure and universal element, one that happened to emanate from every possible skin tone, sexual preference and religious persuasion or lack thereof. From my weekend hedonism to my studies and everywhere in-between, I was deliciously stunned to reveal one after another of the tell-tale and absolutely indisputable signs that within all human beings exists a core of common needs and hopes.

As wonderful as my new lease on life made me feel, quite often I would get disgusted with myself, thinking about how I used to be and the things I had done. I'd sit in class and look around at my classmates—people who I had now come to respect and care for—and wonder how the fuck did I ever want to hurt them. But every time I would get down, there would be a new friend to pick me up, whether they knew it or not.

Of all the classes I took during that time, Charlie Dee's English 201 left the most indelible impression. 201 is essay-writing. The night of the first class Charlie wasted no time, demanding that we all produce 3 hand-written pages of arbitrary essay within a matter of minutes. I was floored along with everyone else, but as the biro gained momentum and the awkward re-introduction to my own handwriting set-in, the chicken-scratched words went from a crawl directly to a run across the college-rule.

I can't remember for the life of me what the topic of that first impromptu essay was, but I do clearly remember Charlie spending the remainder of the class period calling us to the front one-by-one where he brutally dissected what we had managed to write and left the entrails strewn about for everyone else to see. The entire class sat squirming in stunned silence as we watched the first sorry student get their produced-under-duress essay torn to pieces by our instructor. "What the HELL is this supposed to mean?!" "Is that supposed to be a sentence?!" "I have no idea what you're trying to say here and neither would anyone else reading it!"

My own bitch-slapping came somewhere in the middle of the pack. Watching Charlie tear my unfortunate predecessors to bits—some of them appeared to be on the verge of tears and/or socking Charlie in the grill—I felt the conflicting dread of my impending turn, as well as a desire to just fucking get it over with. How bad could it be? Some were getting tooled by the red pen and razor tongue more than others, but everyone got tooled. It was only a question of how bad. Besides, I've been cracked over the head with numerous heavy objects, face down on frozen pavement with the boots of Federal Agents on my back, and felt the whizz of bullets past my ear, among a long list of much more traumatic incidents —how intimidated was I going to be by a scrawny middle-aged English teacher?

By the time my name was called I had passed any fear I was feeling and walked up to his desk with a bit of a smirk, treating the situation like any other fight. Charlie noticed my scrappy approach and dug in to my paper with a renewed zeal for error-detection. He did find enough to dole out an appropriate amount of beratement—at least enough to let the class know that my paper was almost as fucked-up as any of theirs. But my smirk remained as I knew better, and so did he. Our eyes met as I received the paper back from him and I sensed that I would like this guy and his class.

The death-edits marched on until everyone had a turn being eviscerated, then Charlie saddled us with what seemed like an impossible writing regimen as we scurried out the door. English 201 was a summer class, so it met two nights a week and the workload was a semester's worth crammed into a month and a half. I dove into my assignments with relative enthusiasm and came to Thursday night class completely prepared with a draft of my first essay.

There was plenty of room to sit this time, as a good 3rd of the class had dropped after the carnage of Tuesday night. More people would drop the class over the coming week, obviously not responding to Charlie's feet-to-the-fire tactics as positively as I did. By the 3rd week, only a dozen or so students remained out of a class that originally numbered close to 30.

Of the hardy survivors, there was a common feeling of solidarity that we alone possessed the fortitude necessary to endure class after class of ruthless Charlie Dee editing. Charlie himself didn't seem bothered by the attrition rate, and I imagine it wasn't a novel occurrence in his teaching career.

Once the class roster stabilized, we broke-up into smaller groups of 3-4 people where we would read our papers to each other and provide feedback of a much gentler nature than Charlie's.

My group consisted of myself, two middle-aged women from Milwaukee, and a younger African girl. Being the only white person in the mix, not to mention the only guy, was certainly an odd sensation. But primed by my thumping, ecstasy-infused tribal sessions in dirty abandoned warehouses I welcomed it, finally able to appreciate such a learning opportunity. Epossi, the African girl, was fresh from Liberia, with a thick accent and an air of dignity about her that coupled with a beautiful face and body made her quite attractive. My mind reeled at the realization that I found a black woman hot. She vehemently disagreed with my submission for the persuasive paper, "Why Marijuana should be Legalized", citing how the devil weed had made her cousin into a lazy bum. We went back and forth a while, with the other ladies in my group chiming in here and there on both sides of the argument. Though no one had changed their minds about ending marijuana prohibition or not by the end of the class period, I did have a very rewarding feeling of positivity after lively discussion with three people whose viewpoints both refreshed and enlightened my nascent open mind.

By the time we were working together on our final papers, the topic of which was a major turning point in our lives, we had gotten to know each other pretty well. For a moment I wondered if Charlie knew what sort of curveball he was pitching to me with the turning point topic, then I rolled-up my sleeves and got to work knocking it out of the park.

I wrote a paper about who I used to be, and how I came to leave the movement. Sadly, the paper itself was lost amidst shuffles from hard drive to hard drive since then, but I do recall that the gist of it focused on how lovely it was to go and get fucked-up at rave parties instead of getting fucked-up on shite beer by the case and then fucking innocent people up. There was a specific shout-out to the role marijuana played in my reformation of course, not only for the sake of truth (it was), but also for Epossi's sake.

The merits of marijuana aside, I did a fair job of capturing the emotions involved in traveling between such distant poles. I struggled to contain tears as I read the first draft aloud to my new friends. Looking up from behind the paper once I had finished, the tears could no longer be held back as I took in the effect my words had had on my classmates. They were all managing tears of their own, but when my dismay at their reaction was noticed, Mary took one of my hands and Ruth took the other and gave me smiles like that of a mother who has just found her long-lost child. "That's beautiful baby…" "I'm so proud of you!" A sensation of warmth rolled over me not unlike the chemically-induced good times of an ecstasy trip, only it was real.

Epossi was crying as well, but I could sense there was a good deal of anger tangling with the forgiveness that prevailed in the tears of Ruth and Mary. Her anger had nothing to do with smoking pot or not. It had everything to do with how the hell could I go on for so long hating and hurting people for no reason. She had every right to be angry, but she was also a kind enough person to realize that my contrition was indeed genuine.

Wanting to talk more in-depth about my story, but mindful of limited class-time and 3 more drafts to work on, we moved on to Ruth's paper once the tears dried. Her turning point involved divorcing a crackhead husband and kicking him out of the house. I listened to Ruth tell us about how a man she once fell in love with grew enslaved to substance abuse, putting her and her two children through a living hell in the process. He had not only lost his job, but he was prone to hocking anything in the house that wasn't nailed down—including his children's toys—for rock money while Ruth was out working two jobs trying to keep the lights and heat on in their inner city apartment. My fists clenched as she hitched through the part about how he would beat her and the kids as she was scrambling to get them to school and herself to job number one. At that point it had been a good year since I had been in a fight, and up until I saw the pain on Ruth's face I hadn't missed it. But now I sorely wanted to hunt down her shitbag old man and beat him until there was nothing left.

Fortunately there was a happy-ish ending to Ruth's essay; she had obtained a restraining order against him and after being arrested the first few times he came slinking back he finally stopped coming back entirely. When asked of his current whereabouts, Ruth gave an exhausted sigh and said softly and simply, "I don't know. Maybe he's dead...."

All of those years I looked upon black people in the ghetto with disgust and blamed them for turning once-nice neighborhoods into shit, I had of course never stopped to think what it would be like to be born into those conditions. I had lived in those conditions myself, but I did so by choice, spurning the privilege of being born white and middle-class to take on a twisted mission. Listening to Ruth I was struck by an empathy not only for her and her children but for all people living in impoverished drug-riddled violent places. What right did I ever have to pass judgment on people who endure waking nightmares every day? I had no right whatsoever, but back in the day that didn't matter because I didn't look upon Ruth, Mary, Epossi, or anyone else who wasn't "white" as people. I saw them as threats that must be eliminated. Now, thanks to Charlie Dee's English 201, I had learned that they were people indeed, ones that were more genuine and caring than the superfluous suburb-dwellers that I had grown up with. They were people who not only prevailed against imposing odds on a daily basis just to eat and keep warm, but also people who when presented with my miserable past chose to forgive me.

Charlie himself could see the lessons-within-lessons that were hitting me broadside over the course of his class. He and I would stay late and talk, first about ending marijuana prohibition, then about ending racism and promoting social consciousness. Arrangements for after-class beers were even made a couple of times, but never materialized for one reason or another. Regardless, Charlie's class was a vital step in my healing process, and I'll always treasure the experience I had that summer. As it turns out, I'd see Charlie again in the midst of another life-enriching experience...

arno michaelis

11: Obama

Aspiration is the engine of human life. Aspiration in the biological sense of breathing and cellular activity that connote fundamental life, but also, and as importantly, aspiration in the sense of hope. Hope for peace. Hope for compassion. Hope for the Earth. A solid belief in the basic goodness of humanity.

It was the primal theme of hope expressed so beautifully by Barack Obama that led me to become a part of his presidential campaign. Hope for a nation governed by the people and for the people—a nation finally able to realize the sublime graceful strength of its diverse citizens working together to enable their collective and individual dreams.

Every word spoken by then-Senator Obama evoked visions of accomplishing such greatness, and every action of his campaign affirmed the possibility.

I spent election day 2008 walking around Milwaukee's inner city, knocking on doors and talking to every person I met in an effort to land as many Obama votes as possible. One door I knocked on was answered by a young girl who very politely listened to me explain that I was from the Obama campaign and I was just stopping by to see if everyone in the house had voted yet. I asked if her mom or dad was home and she turned back and jubilantly said to her mother, "Mama! The man from Obama is here, and he WHITE!" She would have been less surprised to see an 11 foot-tall Easter Bunny with a Jack-O-Lantern full of Valentines on her doorstep than a middle-aged white guy canvassing for a black presidential candidate.

That moment encapsulated the hope and possibility signified by Barack Obama. There was the sense that after lifetimes of feeling that white people don't care about them, black people finally felt like white people really do care about them. . . and so do Latino people, and Asian people, and gay people, and straight people, and Jewish people, and Christian people, and Muslim people—they all care about them.

And in turn they care about us. "Us" being everyone. There doesn't have to be a "them" anymore.

Later that evening I punctuated the day by joining my fellow campaigners for what we all knew would be a victory party. Perhaps a thousand of the most diverse people I could possibly imagine re-defined the word "celebration" underneath huge widescreens that ticked off the incoming poll results. The party became more raucous and somehow more joyous with each state that went our way.

A stream of exhilarating, cleansing tears began when it was announced that Obama won Ohio—tears that would ebb and flow throughout the night.

I wandered around the posh hotel that hosted the

party, dumbfounded at the sheer variety of people who had worked hand-in-hand for the past year to make this all happen. Human bio-diversity reminiscent of a teeming coral reef or a steamy rainforest that was miraculously sans predation.

The tears running down my face were the same tears shed by the Muslim women wearing hijabs to my right, the young Latina girls to my left, and the enormous prematurely-balding white guy who danced with his toddler son on his shoulders in front of me.

The same tears that ran down the familiar face of the man who helped set me on the path that led to that night —Charlie Dee. We revelled in the sheer rightness of finding each other amidst the triumphant crowd and reminisced about English 201. I hope Charlie is proud of my transformation, as he was a crucial component of it.

I found myself talking to a conservatively dressed older black man named Maurice when Barack Obama's presidency was announced. We embraced in one of the nicest, most pure hugs I've ever had the pleasure of taking part in; two complete strangers from what would be pointed out as vastly different backgrounds prior to that night, now celebrating the wonderful similarities pointed out by our common aspiration.

Aside from the birth of my daughter, I've never felt anything more right than the vibe that night. And I've never truly felt the depth of just how wrong I was back then. . .

arno michaelis

12: déjà vu

We armed ourselves with pistols, shotguns, and assault rifles.

We knew that the government had us impossibly outgunned but nevertheless felt obliged to not only prepare ourselves for the upcoming collapse of society as we had known it, but also to do whatever it took to speed the day when that collapse occurred.

The government was illegitimate; a puppet regime manipulated by a shadowy and sinister force that was hellbent on our destruction. The supposed democracy that seated traitorous politicians had been tainted by mass media that poisoned the minds and souls of our people to not only blind them against what was happening, but also to con them into complicity in their own downfall.

Our guns served many purposes. In addition to the simple purpose they were designed for—to kill people— our firearms endowed us with a sense of destiny befitting an epic struggle against fearsome odds.

The deadly seriousness of the situation was underlined, *italicized*, and **emboldened** by the smell of gun oil and the clack of magazines sliding into position as we recruited new soldiers to our movement.

According to the Founding Fathers, it was not only our right, but our duty to bear arms against the tyrants who had usurped our beloved Nation.

I spent 7 years immersed in that world. A reality where I was constantly looking over my shoulder to reveal the handiwork of the enemy. Every aspect of our culture faced a relentless assault. Everything that was good about America—Life, Liberty, And The Pursuit Of Happiness—had been denigrated and disparaged by those that sought to impose Marxist equality. I hated them for that. I hated them with the passion of a patriot. That hate was fueled by what I truly believed was a love for my race.

Oops! Did I say "race"? I meant a love for my *country*. Or was it a love of Christ? Or Allah? It could have been any of a number of allegiances—any number of ways to identify myself—that I built walls around and bristled at those outside, and it was all in the name of love.

Roads to a lot of really bad places are paved with that kind of bizarro love. A vampiric, soul-depleting love-substitute that beckons to those who never know the real thing.

I was very lucky to realize the true love of a little girl—my daughter—otherwise I'd likely be dead or in prison like so many of my former comrades. Simply by playing with other children, she taught me that the walls and guns and hate that had seemed to give me purpose were in fact unnecessary constructs that threatened to separate us. The children she shared toys, laughs, and smiles with also shared the same need for love and compassion that we all do—regardless of the color of our skin, our family's choice of spirituality, or the part of the world we come from.

I made a decision to cast aside the fear that masqueraded as love, and to live my life in wonderful affection for diversity instead of scorn for it.

But I'll never forget what it was like to hate people.

I wish I could forget. Especially about all of the innocent people I've hurt and motivated others to hurt. I was in a band that made some of the most violent, hateful records ever recorded—records that are still galvanizing racists today. There's no way I can undo the damage I've done. My words have been bellowed loud enough to be encoded into viral digital venom that anyone can come across on the internet. There's no way to take those words and deeds back. However, I can speak in my new voice; one that rails against violence and hatred with an even greater volume.

Events that have taken place since President Obama has been inaugurated concern me deeply. In the eyes of Birthers, Deathers, Town-Hallers, and Tea-Partiers, I see the fiery reflection of who I used to be. While there may be academic differences in the exact nature of the fear that fuels that fire, the core explosive is the same. Those people are ready to pull triggers and defend their bristling walls just as I was. Just as my friends who were murdered or imprisoned were. And the victims are once again innocents—from a security guard at the Holocaust Museum, to a doctor in Kansas, to police officers in Pittsburgh.

I like to hope that somehow the people who are succumbing to fear today will come to their senses as I did. Though I would be more hopeful if there weren't very powerful financial interests inspiring that fear. Unlike back in my hateful days, when armed self-styled militias were looked upon in nigh-universal disdain, those of today are applauded and cajoled by not only widely accepted media mouthpieces, but also by elected politicians. Entities that in my perspective are busily engaged in 5 of the 8 stages of genocide as defined by the United Nations, and all the while concocting a phantom genocide against themselves to justify it.

I by no means wish to silence them; to do so would vindicate their paranoia and further inflame the unbalanced who follow. But it is my onus to point out familiar patterns, and hope that someone listens, and puts their guns down before more people get hurt.

13: war, peace, and BHG

Months past the anniversary of Barack Obama's inauguration, I'm chagrined to admit a significant sense of disappointment. It's easy to look back on the idealism that motivated me during the campaign and feel foolish for ever believing that a Democratic majority controlling the government would produce a different result than the Republicans.

Both sides of the aisle are rife with whores. They cater to a wide range of Johns, but the common thread is the dollar that buys their services. As shady bailouts and continuation of draconian Bush policies are perpetrated by the Obama administration and the Dems fumbling through Congress, the GOP is falling all over itself to point out that 'ol Dubya by no means had a monopoly on such things. As usual, they have nothing constructive to offer, other than impassioned pleas to restore the blatant kowtowing to plutocracy in place of the Democrat's covert subjugation to the same masters.

It's gotten to the point where I can no longer defend Obama's policies, but I do still believe that he is a well-intentioned man for the most part—that he is a basically good human being. He walked into quite a mess and has made genuine attempts at positive change, only to have his efforts gutted and perverted by corporate interests. I will likely campaign for him again in 2012, albeit this time in the sickening "Lesser Of Two Evils" mode instead of buoyed by the wonderful hope that motivated the 2008 victory.

Perhaps what saddens me most is the inclination to acknowledge a precept that served as a cornerstone to my despicable past beliefs; that there will be no peaceful positive change within the confines of the United States Government.

My idea of positive has thankfully evolved from the lowly slug of "a whiter and brighter world" to one of an inclusive society for all human beings, but the rabid dissatisfaction with the powers-that-be remains. It seems the disease that rots D.C. has advanced too far to be cured by anything but a good old-fashioned chug-a-bottle-of-rotgut-whiskey-but-save-some-to-dump-on-the-stump-where-your-limb-was amputation.

But I've been down that road before. I know where it leads. Whether a declaration of war against the government is made in the name of the white race or the human race, war remains the end result.

Have I come this far to give up the dream of peace that took so long to coalesce?

The excruciatingly painful lessons of my past are there to refer to. I can dust off old battleplans and the cold numbness required to execute them—or I can take a deep breath and work to seek positivity in a negative situation.

The fatality of self-fulfilling prophecy is perhaps the most poignant of all the lessons I've learned. It is too easy to acquiesce to outrage. True honor lies not in obliging aggression but in finding the wisdom to fend it off peacefully.

Whether Obama succeeds or fails miserably, the incredible experience I was fortunate enough to be a part of will remain untarnished if I choose to concentrate on the value of the journey itself instead of just the destination. No matter how things shake down, my voice was heard along with millions of others—from all ethnicities and walks of life—who shared the dream of a tolerant, healing nation that seeks a harmony of people and Planet.

Even as I witness the reactionary backlash orchestrated by those in the lucrative business of sowing fear and anger, I reflect on who I used to be and the transformation I've gone through to become a person who lives in spite of strife instead of for it. Whether or not lofty campaign promises are delivered, my belief in a world where people are more important than profit remains genuine.

My past is a demonstration of the human ability to frame reality. Not reality as-in events beyond our control —both sunny days and hurricanes are a bit outside my sphere of influence—but the lens through which reality exists. All of the information a person uses to make decisions and react to events is viewed through that lens. I've proven that one can frame reality to suit the voracious appetite of fear and hate. And maybe for my particular soul that had to be proven before I could envision a more positive reality: one where I'm able to help those who are in danger of falling victim to fear before they make the same mistakes I did.

Every minute you spend hating someone is a hole in your life.

Today I busy myself filling those holes with love. Believing in the basic goodness of humanity—especially the basic goodness of those who seem evil—is how it's done. That primal goodness exists within every human being, whether it is acknowledged or not. Just as the Earth has recovered from countless catastrophes over the billions of years of her existence, the basic goodness of human existence persists, sprouts, and inevitably blossoms in response to suffering.

Human beings naturally abhor seeing other humans suffer. The delusions inspired by fear and ego can cause us to dehumanize almost at will in order to justify that pain. Since we don't care to see our fellow humans suffer, we consciously take their humanity down a notch.

Suddenly the people suffering are somehow less human than we are. We convince ourselves that it has to be that way if we are to obtain the comforts and material we think we need. White lives are more valuable than black lives. American lives are more valuable than

Mexican lives. Christian lives more valuable than Muslim lives. Or vice-versa in endless combinations. This is the root process that leads to slavery, war, and genocide.

So how do we overcome such overwhelming horror? If people are basically good, then why do they do harm? What happened to bring them to that point? These questions won't always have happy-ending answers. But by giving the benefit of the doubt, most often the root causes of violence can be revealed, and thus properly addressed to solve problems instead of simply treating symptoms of an illness.

After living 39 years that saw a disproportionate amount of hatred and violence, and examining what transpired to bring such harm about, I've come to realize that despite the darkest displays of human nature, our core love and compassion for each other is indomitable —like the first sapling to emerge from the ashes of a forest fire. Such wonder lies within every one of us, waiting for the smoke and flame of fear and aggression to clear.

I realize basic human goodness every day when I think well of and for others, especially if they offend me. It's not easy. The practice takes the utmost bravery, because I'm far from perfect and never will be. I still get angry about shit both stupid and serious. I will always struggle with violence, and even though I haven't put my hands on someone for well over a decade, I still beat the hell out of myself emotionally as ongoing punishment for all of the harm I've caused.

But as all of that storms here and there I nurture the warmth of compassion, growing the feeling until it graces more and more of my day, where it will meet other beings and share. And heal. And comfort.

We all have the ability to realize our basic human goodness—the innate and natural desire to live an open and honest life while treating all other life with compassion and respect. This core truth serves as the foundation for peace as it's common to every world religion and transcending of ethnicity, nationality, sexuality, and any other sort of difference that seems to sort human beings.

Once we choose to take that path, and persevere along it's drastic ups and downs, we're able to recognize the true beauty of life. The path that seemed so treacherous becomes joyful and rewarding as we soothe our own suffering by simply loving our great big dysfunctional family—the human race.

epilogue: me and Rob

May 27th, 2010

"Arno, salutations from Kentucky, my name is rob, we never met but I did correspond with you and others in Milwaukee around '88-'89 and so on, the N.H.S-C.O.T.C days, I was from fair oaks, MI. I've read your writings for life after hate, and think my god your story holds a very erie resemblance to my own. I'm no longer a member of any group or club or gang, so don't feel that this is a race-traitor thing, I do have a small group of friends that are active white-nationalist, they are old and true friends. I just wanted to talk to some one who may relate to my life of regret. I held all those guys, those brothers in the highest regard, it took years for me to see the lies and betrayal of those people, it was heart breaking for me. Hammerskin as well as church of the creator, has left me with a police record, alcoholism, broken home for my child, and uneasy feelings in my own family. regards....rob"

"hey Rob,

Your name does sound familiar, but the bulk of my memories from back in the day are fuzzed with booze.

Even stuff like letter-writing was done drunk or hungover.

I'm glad you found our site and also glad that you read my stuff! I really appreciate you taking the time to do that and taking the time to contact me here.

As far as eerie resemblances go, I know exactly what you're saying, and actually, the more people I talk to who were involved with the movement and later had a change of heart, the more the common threads become apparent. Police records, broken homes, alcoholism, and family dysfunction are scars that we all bear to one degree or another. But regardless of degree (I'm not a felon only because I never got caught), bearing these kinds of burdens is a hard thing to deal with. As you may know from my writings, I fled the movement to lose myself in drugs and (more) alcohol. I did do a lot of healing during that time, and the forgiveness and acceptance that new non-movement friends gave to me was a huge part of my turnaround, but it wasn't till I quit drinking in 2004 that I started to seriously think about writing. I started writing a memoir in 2007 and by January of this year the memoir had morphed into Life After Hate and presented itself to the world. Considering that I left the movement in 1995, you can see how long of a process it's been.

And I know what you mean about regret. I still feel it every day in all sorts of ways. I regret that I ever recruited Chuck Miller into the movement, as it led to his death. I regret all the people I've hurt with my hands and all the people the other people I recruited hurt. I regret that Centurion CDs are still being sold and making money for the movement and inspiring kids to hate each other. I regret being drunk or hungover for the first 11 years of my daughter's life. All of these things are super-heavy and I feel like if I didn't get LAH off the ground they may have ultimately dragged my to my grave. Since the MLK Holiday this past January when we launched LAH, I've felt better and better as the guilt and regret has been soothed by the positive experiences I've had. I don't think I'll ever truly shed the stink of what I've done, but if I can effect enough positive change to offset the harm I've caused, I think I can manage to be happy. Hence the Life After Hate mission!

There are a lot more of us than you may think. Guys like T.J. Leyden and Frank Meeink have been traveling the country and talking to kids about the kind of damage the movement does to you since the mid-nineties. I believe that there are many kids who ultimately made some life-saving decisions because of what those guys had to say. I admire them both for that and highly recommend reading their respective books. If you found my writing worthwhile, I think you'd really dig their stuff too.

As far as your friends who are still active; you know as well as anyone what we were capable of doing, so be careful in dealing with them. Don't put yourself in vulnerable positions. I recommend the fade-out, which is basically just hanging out less and less and citing work and family as the reasons. You won't be lying either, as I think you realize by now that if you want a career and a happy family, you need to get the fuck out. I'm sure your friends are good guys, but you probably don't want to put them in a position of choosing you or the movement. If you can sense that any of them want out too, by all means talk to them or send them my way, but you gotta think of yourself and your family first right now. 20 years ago I was the same basically good person I am now, only horribly misguided about my life and the world around me. I honestly believed that the white race was facing genocide at the hands of the Jews, and hell if I was gonna let that happen! I convinced myself and many others that we had no choice. While I loved to fight, I didn't really relish the idea of mass murder, but I thought I was prepared to be a mass-murderer if that's what I had to do to save my race. Now I see that the "genocide" that I was so worried about was really a concoction—a culmination of thousands of years of anti-semitism and centuries of racism.

Today I have friends of every imaginable color. I have friends who are Jewish, friends who are Muslim, friends who are Christian, friends who are atheist, and everywhere in-between. I have gay friends and straight friends. I love them all and each one of them has enriched my life in incredible and unique ways. One of the things that hits me over and over again as I look around me now after looking back at who I was is how much I was missing out on. All the culture, all of the creativity (the real kind, not the COTC kind), all of the beauty and humor I had denied myself because I had written it all off as "mud-race shit" or "Jew shit"... I suppose one of my greatest regrets is that I blacked-out a 7 year chunk of my life during the time I was in the movement. I often wonder what my life would be like if I hadn't made all those mistakes. But ultimately, the life I have in front of me as I type this is the only one that matters, and I'm determined to do as little harm as possible to all the life around me while taking in as much of the moment as I can.

The best advice I can give you is to seek the beauty of the moment you're living in. Cherish each moment you have with your child, each smile, each giggle, even each tantrum, as that kid will be an adult before you know it and those moments will be gone. Set an example for happiness by treating everyone and everything with as much compassion and respect as you can—especially if they seem to not deserve it. In doing so lies true honor and bravery, and a child raised to do likewise will not only be a blessing to the world but will have a rich and rewarding life no matter what happens to them. What better gift could you give as a father?

It's not easy by any means, and it is an ongoing and imperfect process. I still get mad about stupid shit and do mean things to people that I regret. I'm not Gandhi by any stretch! But by learning about great men like him, and trying to follow in their footsteps, I'll live a happier life and make the world around me a little better place every day. Do the best you can and when you fuckup (you will), just learn from it and put it behind you.

Are you still drinking? If so, quitting is another crucial step for turning your life around. You'll be amazed at how much nicer life is without booze. The phrase "High on life" is no bullshit! Just about every day I'm rockin a buzz better than any I've ever got from alcohol or drugs (and believe me, I've done about all of them). Again, it takes a while, and it's hard work, but the reward of sobriety and clarity is fantastic and empowering, not to mention that again, it's a very important example to set for your kid. I stopped on my own, but there's no shame in AA or other counseling, so if you are still drinking, do whatever it takes to stop.

I'm really glad you wrote me man.

Feel free to hit me up anytime on facebook or at mlah@lifeafterhate.com to talk about whatever. I wish the best for you and your family.

-arno"

May 28th

"I've got a lot of conflicting feelings, I have a lot of shame and dislike for myself, cant put the past in the past, Its hard to look at yourself and ask ,was I wrong or has the world gone crazy? I have so much to say, so many questions, do I deserve to be released or do I carry this on my soul until the end? how do you make right with the countless numbers of nameless, faceless people you've left beaten down into the ground, people crying why? .....rob"

"the first thing you need to do is understand that you are a good person Rob. The only way you could have continued to hurt people without giving a shit about it would be if you were a full-blown sociopath. The fact that you've taken the effort to read LAH and contact me reaffirms that you are a good guy, who can be a great father, and a person who can make a positive impact on society. Shame and dislike for yourself will spill over to hurt others. Be cool with yourself. Treat yourself gently, as you love your child.

We were wrong about all sorts of things. There's no need to go into specifics at this point, only to stop hurting people in response to those wrongs. Once you've done that, you have already taken a huge step forward, and a huge step away from your past.

Remember this: the past is gone, the future yet unborn —the right here and now is where it all goes on. (Beastie Boys)

Torturing yourself over things you have done will not help the people you have hurt. That will only make you suffer more and ultimately pass that suffering on to others, who will do likewise to others. Hurting over your past perpetuates the harm you have caused. Treating everyone you can with as much compassion, kindness, and respect that you can will soothe the pain and shame you feel, as well as bring a little happiness to others. All life is interconnected. Your actions will cause chain-reactions that can be good or bad. If you're on the way to work and in a bad mood and you scowl at the guy who works at the gas station as you pay for your gas, he's gonna think, "wtf is that guy's problem?!" and likely carry that negative vibe with him, laying it on someone else, and so-on. Ultimately, someone is gonna come home and beat their wife, or child, or do some kind of needless harm to someone else. Their victim will seek to retaliate somehow, and the cycle of suffering continues.

You can remove yourself from that cycle simply by smiling at everyone you see. It's really that easy to begin making a positive impact. Try it for a day and see how good it feels. Most people will smile back at you then pass it on. Some people will be stuck in their own bullshit, but since you're smiling you don't have to take their problems on and pass them on. Take it a step further by holding the door for people young, old, rich poor, black, white, whatever. Little acts of courtesy and respect like that are immensely powerful, and will do wonders to improve your mood.

Practice kindness and respect as often as you can. You don't have to continue the hate by hating yourself. Being nice to people and thinking of others before you think of yourself is how you can release the burden of guilt you bear. You don't have to continue to suffer.

Down the road maybe you can find some place to

volunteer to help people who need it. Soup Kitchens are good. So is Habitat for Humanity. There are a ton of organizations out there that help people who need it. Finding one that you can really engage with is a great way to feel better about yourself and the rest of the world. You could go the route that many of us are and reach out to organizations that promote peace, taking to people about where you were and helping them to not make the same mistakes. Don't rush to do that though. If that's something that is for you, you'll know when the time is right.

For now, just concentrate on treating all life with as much kindness and respect as you can muster. That will definitely help you feel better and jump-start the process of moving forward."

June 1st

"arno, regards, If I had to give up booze living in this crazy city, in this crazy state, in this crazy country,in this crazy world, I might kill myself!"

"heh! I can relate man.

but I'm here to tell ya life is better without it, and you should think long and hard about how your drinking effects your kid and your ability to be a father. I won't hassle you any more about it though. If you ever feel like you need to stop, you'll stop."

june 15th

"Did you ever have trouble with one group of friends thinking that you've become a race-traitor and another group thinking that you are just the same ol' nazi-thug trying to put a new spin on nationalism? I have spent the better part of the last ten years getting my name off of mailing list and contact list because of all the wackos that the cause had attracted and how many guys took on the biker-gang type mentality, I think in doing that i've lost some good friends but at the same time I turned my back on a lot for doing the very same. If I told you that part of me didn't miss the comradeship of close brothers, I'd be lying. Regards, rob"

"I totally know how you feel Rob. I go through it every day. As I go around promoting LAH just about everyone I talk to is like, 'this is awesome! We really want to work with you and do this this and that...' and then I never hear from them. The first thing I think is that I said something to piss them off, or they don't like me for some other reason. Then I get pissed and think 'here I am trying to make amends for what I've done and they don't even appreciate it!' and shit goes downhill from there. But when I really examine my thought process, it's clear that all the drama exists in my head—in the way that I'm interpreting things. Yeah, some people are gonna think you're too far right and some will think you're too far left but the question that needs to be asked is; are you being honest with yourself? That's what really matters. Once you break everything down, once you can set aside all the dogma, you'll see what's left is your need to be treated with kindness and respect. Every single human being on this planet has that need. And every single human being has the ability to accommodate that need.

I know as well as anyone that you don't just flip a switch and start caring about people. It's a gradual process, but the further you get into it the easier it becomes to show compassion for life. And the more rewarding it becomes.

As far as friends go, you need to think about whether they would be your friend no matter what. Would they be your friend if you didn't quite fit the mold created by the ideology. That goes for racists and anti-racists alike. When I was on my way out of the movement, there were some guys who were pretty heavy-hitters who I was really tight with that I used to drunk-dial all the time and talk about non-movement stuff like family and relationships, and even stuff that was forbidden like football and Seinfeld. They knew I was having doubts, but they were my friends first and white power activists second. I don't talk with anyone active nowadays. The guys I'm thinking of may or may not still be active. Considering the public stance against racism that I've taken, I don't know that I would trust them if they were still active, but when I was on the way out, they just let me do my thing rather than try to rope me in or attack me. That was yet another indicator to me how wrong what we were doing was. When it came down to it, friendship was more important than 'saving the white race'

I have a lot of friends who are as opposed to the movement as I am now. Both Pat O'Malley and Christian Picciolini were as deeply involved in the movement as I was and both of them are still close friends today. I guess what I'm saying is that if they really are your close brothers, that's a bond that exists above and beyond the movement. If they don't accept you unless you toe the line ideology-wise then it's plain that they don't really care about you, they only see you as a warm body for cannon-fodder in a pointless and futile war against reality. Don't let yourself be used.

I was very lucky to run into a group of new friends that accepted me and forgave me. It can be hard to find people like that who put people first and ideology second. I know a lot of leftys (and I'm pretty far left myself) who have zero tolerance for anyone to their right, and that's no better than Rush Limbaugh having zero tolerance for anyone to his left (pretty much everyone). I had a great talk with T.J. Leyden last Friday. Though we didn't quite see eye-to-eye politically, we both clearly agreed that people are better off when we treat other well. That simple. So my advice would be to take inventory of the people in your life who can agree on that and spend more time with them and less with those who's respect for you depends on treating people like shit.

Let me know if any of that made sense! ...and it's great to hear from you. Hit me up any time Rob.

Peace my brother,
-arno"

arno michaelis

In Loving Memory
of the friend who shared my birthday.

His 18th was his last.

Appendix A: Riverwest Interview

In the beautiful late summer of 2008, a friend introduced me to a sociology PhD candidate who was working on her dissertation about Milwaukee's Riverwest neighborhood. Sandwiched between the perpetually fashionable East Side and the severely depressed North Side, Riverwest was the setting for my descent from lowly angst-ridden punker to even lower racist skinhead. Sandy and I hit it off and she did a great job of leading the interview, which turned out to be a condensed if not necessarily concise telling of my story.

Sandy: So I would just like to get to know you a little bit. Are you from the area? Where did you grow up?

Arno: I grew up in Mequon, which is a far cry from Riverwest.

Sandy: I grew up in Whitefish Bay.

Arno: Alright. But you can still catch a bus in Whitefish Bay though.

Sandy: Important distinction, I like the way you think.

Arno: As a teenager, I despised Mequon and I despised Homestead High School. I was always a kind of iconoclast and I would go against the grain at every opportunity, even if the grain made sense to me and even if I kinda liked it. It was just counter-intuitive for me to go with the flock, and Mequon is very much the flock [laughs] of society. As early I could I started going to Milwaukee. In middle school I was an early adopter of hip-hop culture and fashion before it was a popular thing to do. I hung out with a lot of black kids, and I went to Starlight Roll-Arena by Northridge Mall to do breakdance battles. I was really immersed in the mid-eighties hip-hop explosion a little bit before it happened. My younger brother and I went to see Run-DMC at the Eagles club in 1984 and it was awesome. We were probably the only white kids there and we were completely comfortable. My mom was a bit nervous but ultimately brave enough to drop off her two sons downtown to see Run-DMC at a time when it was kind of unheard of for white kids to be doing such stuff—unheard of in Mequon at least.

Sandy: What was the initial pull? What got you started on this path because in Mequon—

Arno: The skinhead thing?

Sandy: No, the hip-hop thing.

Arno: People who don't live in Mequon don't get this, but there are areas that are relatively poor compared to Lac du Cours, the Villa du Parks—the really snooty subdivisions. There are some areas that are much more middle class, and that's where the black kids lived. I have

—

Sandy: So you are connecting with kids in your neighborhood?

Arno: Yeah. I had a group of friends that was me and couple other white kids, a Filipino kid, and then a bunch of black kids. Jason was probably the richest of the bunch and every weekend we would be in his basement rec-room renting VCR copies of Beat Street and Breakin' and just rolling them over and over again trying to learn the moves, teaching ourselves to breakdance. My mom, who had done some ballet in her college time and was—and still is—very sincerely interested in anything multi-cultural—she thought the whole breakdancing thing was great. There were these kids on Mitchell Street (Milwaukee's South side) who—I should remember the name of their crew—they had a b-boy crew, and they would give breakin' lessons and it was in the back of some dilapidated store and seriously on cardboard and super old school—and my mom brought us down there and paid them 20 bucks or whatever and we were taught some back-spin moves and floorwork stuff—it was the most awesome thing ever.

Then Andy—one of my black friends in Mequon—his older sister went to Starlite all the time, so when we could—and she really didn't want us hanging around with her—but when we could finagle a ride we would get out there and we loved it. When we first started going to Starlite people still roller-skated but after a year or so they opened up the entire roller skating floor to breakdancing because that's all that was going on there. But at the same time there was a lot of gang problems and violence and I think that's what ultimately caused Starlite's demise—just people getting out of hand and not being there to breakdance.

There was kind of a defining moment that was basically the end of my whole breakdancing career in 7th grade. For most of 6th grade and 7th grade, I was really into it and I thought I had a pretty tight-knit group of friends. My whole life I have been really extroverted and never had a problem meeting friends. I was fairly popular but I was also a really cocky prick and a lot of the jock-type guys absolutely hated me. Even though I played football with them and was as good as they were—but I was obviously not a jock. And being the kind of rebel breakdancer guy, I was pretty popular with the girls, which made them like me even less. Later on in 7th grade I had the breakdancer trademark of the time, which was the long rat-tail hairdo. You gotta have that. So one day at recess—in the middle of the playground with all the teachers watching—20 or so jocks came and tackled me, beat me up, held me down, and cut off my tail. And while this happened, all of my homeboys pretty much just stood there—they certainly weren't jumping in on my side, and I felt like… I don't like making this comparison because I don't like to cheapen what a rape victim would go through, but it was a similar experience on my end. I mean, that's kind of how it felt.

Sandy: And public. Like public violation and humiliation.

Arno: Yeah. Exactly. It was pretty rough, but I was a pretty rough kid. I mean I could handle myself but I couldn't fight off 20 dudes—so that was the other thing too, the element of being defeated—regardless of how many of them there were, I just couldn't deal with that. That was a really traumatic thing and I was really disappointed that all my guys didn't do a damn thing to help me out. If one or two of them would have made some kind of resistance, I'd like to think the teachers on the playground could have stopped it. It just kind of went down and it seemed like nobody wanted to help me. After that I still hung out with some of the same kids, but I wasn't really into the breakdance thing anymore—also coinciding was the downhill slide of Starlite. So all these factors kind of merged to create an environment where I got out of the b-boy scene.

Sandy: You phased out.

Arno: Right. And I got into the whole punk thing by the time I was in high school and sophomore year marked a very obvious difference. Up until freshman year I always got pretty much straight A's without putting a whole lot of effort into it. But the summer before sophomore year I started hanging out with much older —sometimes guys in their 30's—punks who had bands going and I started doing DIY shows.

Sandy: Where did you find them in the first place?

Arno: The bands?

Sandy: No, just the people to connect with.

Arno: At shows. Yeah. I think the first punk show I went to was at Echo Bowl [laughing].

Sandy: Blocks from my house.

Arno: Heh! The band was called Earth Shoe. [laughing] And they were awesome. I remember I was like "yeah! Earth Shoe!" …and what the hell is an "Earth Shoe?" My mom said it was some kind of shoe in the 70's, something hippies wore.

Sandy: I still think they exist actually [laughing].

Arno: I'm sure they are quite stylish. So that was my introduction. I loved the music. I loved the attitude. I loved the rebellion and it really spoke to me. I immersed myself in it as much as I could. I feel like I am a lot more introverted now than I used to be, but throughout high school and up into my 30's I was always so gregarious and in some cases obnoxious, that whatever the scene, when I was there everyone knew it and everyone knew who I was—so I made a lot of friends quickly.

I also made a lot of enemies. There were always people who were like "I hate that guy!" [laughing]. I don't blame them, I am sure it was justified. But that's kind of how I got into the punk scene. I got in tight with a whole crew of punks from West Bend and their band. I would go to all their shows and parties up there. I also got in really tight with the punk scene in Kenosha and Racine. If anyone would ever do a dissertation on the Wisconsin or even Midwest punk scene, the Kenosha scene from the early 80's was an integral part—it was huge. There were all kinds of bands and there was hundreds of punks and it was really crazy times. It was a dysfunctional family atmosphere—we're gonna to go smash society together and do a ton of drinking and drugs and everything else.

So as a 14 year-old kid, I was hanging out with all these people and loving every minute of it. I was dragged reluctantly kicking and screaming back to Homestead High School for sophomore year and that's when my grades plummeted, because I stopped doing anything at all.

Sandy: Right, no investment in that world.

Arno: Exactly. None whatsoever. My grades all went to shit. I was getting into as close to physical confrontations with teachers as I could. I was always pushin' them and asking them to take a swing at me and they wouldn't. After sophomore year I organized a tour for my band friends from West Bend. The band was called N.O.D., which stood for Nuclear Overdose. Through Maximum Rock n' Roll and other kinds of… looking back I don't understand how any of this worked without the internet but apparently it did somehow [laughing]. It's kind of a shame now because kids today will never experience what it was like back then. They try. There's still punk stuff that goes on, but I can't look at it and say "it's punk"…but I am digressing.

I set up this tour for N.O.D. I was dating a girl from Indianapolis. I met her while she was up here for a show. The tour was supposed to play in Chicago, Indianapolis, Muncie, Dayton, and then all the way out to Pennsylvania. I had probably—I don't know—6 or 7 gigs set up. I think at the time I really didn't understand the nature of setting up a gig—but I talked to club owners and would say, "Yeah, I got this band…" I sent them tapes, I said "we'll come out and play this day" and they were like, "ok cool, we'll see you then". Honestly, I don't think they really gave a rat's ass if we showed up, they were just shooing us in on a punk night or whatever.

The whole thing ended up a disaster. The Chicago show fell through. We got down to Indianapolis to my girlfriend's house. Her mother was Mexican and didn't speak any English and her dad was points unknown. So me and these two vanloads full of punk-rockers show up at her mom's house and moved in for a couple of weeks [laughs]. Every day she would be going off on us in Spanish and we would like [laughing]—let it flow over us as we would drink and do whatever.

The rest of the shows fell through and I forget the particulars of how, but I am sure it was due to my shoddy promoting. We were stuck in Indianapolis because we went down there without any money. We were planning on making money at these shows for gas. The whole tour turned into a two-week couch trip for 14 people at this poor girl's mom's house [laughing]. We finally, by hook or by crook, scraped up enough money to get back to Wisconsin and when we did, my mom, dad, and younger brother were all out of town. I had just went off on tour with this band saying, "I don't know when I am coming back" and they were like, "alright whatever." At that time they had completely lost control of me, and they had kind of given up on trying to reel me in. We happened to get back the day they left, so—

Sandy: Left where?

Arno: Left our house to go and visit my relatives in California. They were all gone and I had the run of my parents' house in Mequon for two weeks. Of course we had a two week-long rager with all the bands from Kenosha coming up and playing in the basement. I was renting out my parents bedroom [laughing really hard] and I mean the house just got absolutely demolished. My brother, to this day, has not forgiven me for it. My parents kind of have, but my brother is like "I can't believe you did that to your own house! I mean it was our house!" He is still pissed at me about it, that's how messed up it got. There were guys with the lawnmower out in the middle of the night and messing with the deck so it was carving big swaths of dirt in the lawn [laughing]. Broke every dish, ate every piece of food. What we didn't eat ended up on the walls or ceiling. Knee-deep in beer cans and whatnot. This was all going on and I'm just loving it, and finally it dawns on me that they are getting home the next day. And I'm thinking, "we have to get the hell out of here!" —so I took off to Racine where I kind of squatted in this biker's basement with one of my punk-rock friends.

I was there for a month or so when my mom finally tracked me down. She drove down there to get me, and I basically said, "I'm not going back to school. I have had it with school." So my mom being practical said, "well I will get you a job, since you are not going to high school", and I got a job printing t-shirts for a friend of hers who printed bootleg rock shirts—unlicensed—he was raided by the feds all the time [laughing]—that's a story onto itself. And that's when I moved to Riverwest.

Sandy: Why Riverwest?

Arno: Some guys I knew from the punk scene had all gravitated to a house on 700 E. Wright Street, which is still on the corner today. It looks much nicer now than it did back then, and I am surprised there is anything left of it—because we literally tore that house down. We tore the doors off, smashed through the walls—we absolutely gutted it. But that's when I first moved to Riverwest, and I don't know why they originally chose that location—but looking back, the diversity of that neighborhood was pretty much lost on me. I was like whatever, it's a place to party. It's where all the punks are going. That's were I wanted to be. There were two older guys (from my perspective) in their early 20's who were going to UWM —they got the lease, and I would imagine the reason was it was cheap.

Sandy: It still is. And it's not as cheap as it was, but it's still a factor in what brings people.

Arno: Exactly, it's kind of the poor man's East Side. It's cheap. It's in a cool part of town. There is kind of a artistic element to it, and I think that's what led the older guys who got the house to the neighborhood. As far as I was concerned, I was just elated to be striking out on my own. When I should have been going to my junior year of high school, I was printing tee-shirts full-time 3rd shift and living with 5 roommates in this tiny little house and it was the best thing ever. I just worked and I drank, and I went through my normal impact on the scene as I was crashing around.

Sandy: Can I just ask what did it mean to you to be in this scene? What did this scene mean to you when hanging out with punk kids in this house? What was punk to you at this point?

Arno: I was actually on the tail end of my whole involvement with punk scene, and it was the tail end for a number of reasons; one of which is I had made as many enemies as friends so there were whole divisions of the punk scene that hated me. There was a group of kinda proto-skinheads on the South side called the South Side Pride. The band The Crusties, who were the godfathers of Milwaukee punk, were really tight with these guys. And none of them liked me. I mean I was really obnoxious, they didn't like that I just showed up and all of a sudden everyone knew me and everyone liked me and so they all wanted to kick my ass pretty much at any given time.

That's also when I first met Pat O'Malley. I was at a show at the Odd Rock and it was just a really bad night. It was all South Side Pride guys and they were all eye-balling me and waiting to jump me outside and I was getting kinda nervous. Then I met Pat there and we kind of hit it off. I was just starting to get with the whole skinhead thing, too. I was shaving my head but I wasn't officially a skinhead at that point. Pat just said, "so what's up?" and I was like, "yeah, all these dudes are after me" and he said, "yeah, I got your back man, we'll see what they really want to do." Pat then, as he is now, was a really intimidating guy. He's not the hugest guy but he's really intense—he starts barking in your face and you don't want to get involved with him in an adversarial fashion. And he could back it up too. He was a wrestler growing up and he was just really, really tough. So that's where I first met Pat when I was at odds with these guys.

I also had arranged a number of DIY shows that were fairly successful. We would always pack the places. I always took whatever money I got after we paid the place and gave it to the bands and bought beer and rocked out. That's how I first started hanging out with the Kenosha guys—we did a show on New Year's Day—which they were all griping about, as you can imagine—but they came out anyway and it ended up being a huge show. It was at the OddRock and we made a lot of money by teenage punk-rock standards.

After the show, I jumped in the van with those guys and went down to Kenosha, and what money I had—which was a couple hundred bucks—was all beer for everybody and we had a big raging party. For a long time, that's kind of how I was involved with the punk scene, but then I got a little distance from the Kenosha guys and I started hanging out with Pat more often and some of the guys on the Eastside who were more skinheady. I think as I started hanging out with them more, I would hang out with the Kenosha guys less.

Another big factor about leaving the punk scene was that at that time, there was a good chunk of the punk kids who were real left-oriented "peace punks", as we called them—really activist people. It's ironic that now I agree with a lot of what they said, but at the time, they really irritated the fuck out of me. I mean—

Sandy: Both them and their politics?

Arno: Yes. Because of them, I came to despise the politics. I was always the kind of punk that was more anarchist—just break stuff, just destructive, good-for-nothing punk—that's what I was into. So when I saw these people saying, "Don't buy Coors beer because they don't hire black people", I would be like, "Really? O.K." and I would buy Coors beer exclusively, and I would wear a Coors hat to shows just to be a dick. These people obviously didn't like me any more than I liked them, but it was really getting more and more prevalent. It is hard to put my finger on what I hated so much about it. I think, again, it just goes back to because it was popular. It seemed like the popular thing to do amongst punks was to get all political and to start giving a rat's ass about something [laughs], and that just really bothered me. That's one of the things that kind of wedged me away from the punks and more hanging out with the skinheads.

Sandy: What was the appeal there, at that time. What are we 15 now?

Arno: Um, 17. Yeah. I was sort of on my own just railing against the peace punks, and at the time in New York there was a kind of spin-off skinhead movement from the original skinheads in Britain. The New York crews all revolved around a couple of bands like the

Cro-Mags and Agnostic Front. They weren't by any means racist but they were mildly nationalist, and they were sort-of right wing—I mean to the point of not being left, at least. It's funny now when I grow up and understand that right-wing is really old rich white guys who would have absolutely nothing to do with skinheads from New York.

Sandy: Here. That isn't where right-wing means everywhere.

Arno: That's a good point. I guess that's from my Mequon perspective [laughing]. I wasn't really attracted to the politics really, but I liked that these New York guys were huge and covered in ink and really mean and scary looking. I wanted to recreate that in a style of my own, and that's how that kind of started. I would run into these other kids who had gotten into the skinhead thing on their own in one way or another.

A girl I marginally knew drove a van for some punk band all over the country and she ended up in New York where she was really getting sick of how dirty punk rockers were—they were just disgusting to her. Then she met these kids wearing nice shirts that they would button-up and tuck-in their pants. They had Fred Perrys and their boots, and it was just more stylish. So she was initially drawn to the whole skinhead thing because they were stylish, [laughing] and attractive. I think she was dating one too—that was a big part of it. She worked her way back to Milwaukee and along the way she went through Chicago where the Chicago Area Skinheads

(CASH) were one of the first, if not THE first, racial skinhead groups in the country. Through some transient skinhead friends of hers she was introduced to them and it really struck a chord with her. She felt that National Socialism made a lot of sense and these people really have something to say—that there is something to them. Then she came back to Milwaukee, brought Pat back down to Chicago, and her and Pat got into it.

Soon after that, there was a another defining moment; I remember being outside of a show and she flagged me down, "Hey Arno, come listen to this!" and she had a walkman with Screwdriver on it. Screwdriver is the legendary granddaddy skinhead band from England. A really good band actually. They started out as kind of a punk band—I still listen to the punk stuff, it's fantastic —but real quickly they got involved with the overtly racist National Front over there and their music, lyrically, went to all stuff about blood and honor and race and nation. They covered "Tomorrow Belongs To Me" which was a Hitler youth song.

The power of music cannot be overstated. When she put the headphones on me and I heard Screwdriver, I had this feeling of, "...yeah." It was like a light bulb went off and from that moment I was really, really into it. The Chicago guys at the time had a record label where they would import Screwdriver because it was really hard to get otherwise, and it was all a network of P.O. Boxes. The record label that they was called Romantic Violence, which to this day I think is an awesome name. I mean, it's pretty scary.

Sandy: It's pretty powerful.

Arno: Yeah, powerful is the right word. It's just, wow...

Sandy: But if you think about it, is violence that far from here [points to heart]?

Arno: Well right, exactly. That's where it all comes from. That's how I felt about the music. Another appeal of the skinhead thing—the whole idea of nationalism, especially national socialism and racialism was absolutely despised in the punk scene [laughs]. So while I was joining one crew and following in that sense, at the same time I was still railing against the one I didn't like. It was a real natural thing to happen because you know of course my old punk rock friends wouldn't talk to me anymore—and my skinhead friends would say, "that's because they are communists and we have to fight against the communists." And then I figured, "yeah, yeah we do" and it seemed to make a lot of sense to me at the time. That's how I went from a punk to a skinhead.

I should say—this has been illuminated more and more as I'm in the process of writing—that my initial attraction to become a skinhead was purely the need to lash-out at the world. At the time I could really give a shit about black or white or whatever. I was just overjoyed when I realized the impact that running around with swastikas had. I loved how it really pissed people off. I had no consideration for the Holocaust and the real horrors that happened in Nazi Germany. I had no understanding of it and it never really crossed my mind. All I knew was that now it was me and my friends against the world and that's how I liked it.

Sandy: The symbolic power of repelling the masses.

Arno: That's a good way to put it. Absolutely. And it's a self-fulfilling prophecy; when you put a t-shirt on with a big swastika on it that says "WHITE POWER" and go walking down the street and everyone hates you, you are like, "See! See! They all hate the white man!" [laughing] and especially—

Sandy: So that just feeds the fire.

Arno: Sure, yeah. And in Riverwest, being a pretty diverse neighborhood, you know there was plenty of action. My whole life I have always gotten in fights. I have always liked getting into fights. In grade school I would get in school-yard fights, fight the jocks. As a punk, we would fight jocks all the time. In Madison, we would get in brawls with entire fraternities. It was something that I just really got a charge out of doing. If you are really getting into the psychoanalysis bit, I am sure I was trying to fill some void in my life with it, trying to empower myself via physical violence or whatever.

Sandy: Taking away other people's power.

Arno: Yes. So there I was walking down the street with a white power shirt and—surprise—the black guys in the neighborhood don't like it too much and then there are fights with them. That's a self-fulfilling prophecy. So then everywhere I went, any time I saw black people there was tension, if not actual violence.

Sandy: Were you still living in Riverwest at the time?

Arno: Yeah.

Sandy: Were you still on Wright Street?

Arno: Yep.

Sandy: Were you the odd man out at that house?

Arno: Well there was a bunch of us. There was a kind of transition that went on at the 700 Club. When I moved in it was all punkers. I think I was the only skinheady type in there. As things went on, Pat started hanging around more often and a lot of the West Bend guys got into the whole skinhead thing and they shaved their heads and wore flight jackets, it's a bunch of skinheads at the house. That alone kind of drove some of the punk guys out. And the ones that didn't get the hint initially were—

Sandy: Escorted?

Arno: Yeah, we would just be dicks until they wanted to leave. Some of the things were kind of comical. Everybody that lived there was absolutely ass-broke. Everyone was penniless and one of the punk guys—his name was Mike McQueen—does that ring a bell?

Sandy: No, I just think that's just a really great name.

Arno: It is a great name. He was actually a cool guy— there are so many people in the punk scene that I miss and I feel bad about because I really betrayed them all. I went and just totally changed my colors and all these people who I had been really close with I just said, "fuck you, w these transient ones who would stay all over the country and this was all arranged via P.O. box communication.

Sandy: But when in Milwaukee the 700 Club was it?

Arno: Exactly. These people knew who to go find and they would turn up at the 700 Club—and so much happened there. I could talk about the 700 Club all afternoon, but the reality was I lived there from September of 1987 until maybe February or March 1988, so I mean we weren't even there that long. All this took place in a fairly short time span. By the time we were leaving there were nightly, rager—like how much drunker can we get compared to last night, how much crazier can we get—type parties. We would rip the doors off the hinges and we were sliding down the stairs on them and we were kicking holes in the wall—we literally tore the house down. I really have to figure out what the moment was when we realized we better get the hell out of there, but that day came. We all kind of dispersed and just disappeared and the poor guy who owned the house came to find it completely gutted.

Sandy: Do you remember during that time who your neighbors were, or what they were up to? Was there confrontation, or were you guys in your own "fuck you" universe?

Arno: There was a lot of confrontation. I used to walk down to the Polish Falcon because they would serve me there. I got served a lot when I was 17 and I don't know if I looked old but a lot of times I would tell them I was in the military with the shaved head. I would go drinking at the Polish Falcon and usually while I was there I would try to keep things pretty low key, but at the same time we were making so much ruckus and being such a disturbance in the neighborhood that anywhere we went, somebody would see us and say, "You are one of those assholes who live on the corner at Wright Street!" And then some shit would go down...

Sandy: What does that mean?

Arno: Um, verbal arguments and usually our response was, "Yeah, what are you going to do about it? You wanna go outside!?" Then there would be a fight, and sometimes there was ten of them and two of us and sometimes it was vice versa. There was a fairly good range of people who didn't like us—pretty much everybody didn't like us.

Sandy: Diverse yet united in their dislike of you [laughing].

Arno: Heh!. Interesting point. There were the black people who didn't like us, the kind of strange older middle aged white people who didn't like us, and uh— the strange younger people in Riverwest who didn't like us. In any combination, those groups would be there to, you know—provide us what we were really looking for. And when it comes down to it, if we would have been embraced with open arms and people would have bought us beers and been nice to us—despite what kind of assholes we were—it would have really diffused the whole damn thing. We would have had to go find our conflict somewhere else, because the whole skinhead way of life—it requires conflict as a gasoline.

Sandy: That's what I was thinking—fuel.

Arno: Yeah. It operates on conflict and if you don't have it, you don't go anywhere—nothing happens. It just stagnates and the real world starts creeping in and the whole appeal of the "us" against the world thing starts to crack and fade away then what's the point of doing it?

Sandy: So it was kind of understood that you were always looking for it. To create it if it wasn't going to be created or started?

Arno: Yeah. There were a number of times—and these people really annoyed me—but looking back, I can tell they were wiser people who would see us all and would obviously disapprove, but they were smart enough to know that—

Sandy: Confrontation was your food?

Arno: Right. Exactly. And they didn't give it to us. That would really aggravate me [laughing], "What do you mean? We're Nazi's, come on, you don't wanna fight?" and they'd be like, "Whatever... little kids." But they wouldn't even go that far, because they wouldn't spur us on, they would turn the other cheek and not give us what we wanted.

Sandy: And what about cops? Were they ever called? This is before my time in Riverwest.

Arno: Good question. It's actually interesting; I don't recall a single incident where we had any police problems for anything that happened in Riverwest. Any beatings, fights we got into in Riverwest—and there were some really violent ones—nothing ever came back to us cop-wise. There were a lot of arrests but they all stemmed from when we crossed the river to the East Side. When we went to Downer Avenue—when we would cause trouble over there. Whenever that would happen, that's when the cops came looking for us. And yeah...

Sandy: That says so much.

Arno: It totally does. I know exactly what it says. At the time I didn't. As we were taking over the 700 Club, there were some skinhead-types who weren't into the racial thing at all, and they kind of gravitated together and hung out on the East Side on Downer a lot. They called themselves "Brew City Skins", and we called them "Baldies". According to us you couldn't be a skinhead if you weren't white power.

Sandy: What were you guys?

Arno: We were just skinheads.

Sandy: I mean did you have a name?

Arno: Yeah, we were the Skinhead Army of Milwaukee.

Sandy: Wow.

Arno: Yeah. According to us, if you weren't white power, you weren't a skinhead. Never mind that the first skinheads included black guys and that there were Jamaican influences. We were told that, of course. And we were like, "Whatever, that's just Jewish propaganda."

We always had an answer for everything like that. But these non-racist (pause) skinheads—and to this day I have a hard time calling them skinheads because I'm so conditioned, "They're not skinheads, they're baldies."— they all hung out on the Eastside and on Downer Avenue, and we would go looking for them. And every single time we got in a fight with them they would call the police.

Sandy: They would?

Arno: Yeah, they would call the police and press charges against us. It was infuriating, but at the same time, it justified everything we did. It just showed us how much tougher we are than them, that we are not the ones calling the cops, they are.

Sandy: And who were the cops to you? How did you feel about cops?

Arno: They were agents of the Zionist Occupational Government.

Sandy: Can you translate that?

Arno: [laughing]. The common dogma to any white racialist organization is that the United States Government is merely the puppet regime for some world-wide Jewish network that really calls the shots. So that's what we looked at the cops as, and any other figures of authority and whatnot. It was at 700 Club where the Milwaukee gang squad first started coming around. They would wear plain clothes—they knocked on the door one night, and we opened the door and it was this tall dorky white guy and this short older white woman and we were like, "yeah?" and they knew all our names. He said "Hey Arnie, I am Jim Klisch". He and Susan Powers came knocking on our door one night— and this was in late 1987, when it was pretty obvious that this whole skinhead thing was gravitating and going on. When they first walked in and introduced themselves, we said, "What do you guys want?" and they replied, "Oh, we just uh—know you, seeing how you are doing, seeing what's going on, we understand there is a skinhead thing…" and we had no clue how that kind of law enforcement operated. You know, cops show up and arrest you, or they don't. What do you do when they are just talking to us? That was really weird. We would talk to them and ramble on, "Blah, blah, blah, the white race, the Jews…" [we would be rattling off to them and they would just sit there soaking it in. It wasn't until months later that we realized how unwise it was to be running your mouth about anything with cops. They would make periodic visits every couple of weeks or so. But they never came in and, you know, raided the place—they never…

Sandy: And didn't it change your behavior?

Arno: No not at all.

Sandy: They didn't seem like a threat.

Arno: Actually they made us feel like kind of, "Heh! Yeah! Look at that! We got the gang squad coming— now we are big time!" Its funny because when I was interviewing Jim for the book, I asked him, "You know at the time when you were paying attention to us, what was the rest of Milwaukee like gang wise? What was gang activity like in the rest of the city?" And he said, "It was off the hook. There were all kinds of shootings and homicides and drug dealing going on." So I said, "Okay, so you guys had people dedicated to a group of kids who shaved their heads and spray painted swastikas on mailboxes and beat up people once and a while?" and he replied, "Oh yeah", and he knew exactly what I was getting at. But the point is that there was other areas of Milwaukee that were in much more dire need of attention from law enforcement than we were. But it's such a political hot button thing.

Sandy: Like the cost of ignoring you would be too great? Is that what you mean? Like politically?

Arno: I guess that's—

Sandy: Or it was better to be on something?

Arno: I think it's a matter of when you are coming out as a white racist, for political reasons the powers that be have to show that they are doing something. Even if there isn't a logical practical reason to be doing something, they have to be out there to show that they are on it. I kind of see merit to that. To this day—and I hope I have a better answer someday—but I really don't have an answer to say, "this is what you do about Nazis". I know what you don't do. You don't give them conflict, you don't fuel their fire.—[waitress interruption 59:50] When people are violent and are hurting other people you have to stop them but, at the same time, when there's these relatively harmless skinheads, who are just a

179

bunch of kids drinking and carrying on, and 10 blocks away, there's people killing each other and huge amounts of cocaine being thrown around, which is the fire you send the trucks too?

Sandy: Right. But also, how much of violence is physical? And does violence come in other forms and does it have other kinds consequences. I am not trying to say that people killing each other—that that scale doesn't make sense, but it makes it complicated. Because sometimes you are responding to more than people getting beat up.

Arno: That's a good way to put it. It certainly was complicated.

Sandy: And I mean, I'm sure to a lot of people you were threatening—whether or not it's any reality—their ideal of a way of life. Which people freak out about.

Arno: And rightfully so. There are people who actually themselves or had family that went through what happened in Europe and WWII and how are those people supposed to feel when there's dickheads walking around with swastikas down the street? I can see why it would merit a greater degree of attention because of that. But at the same time, it got to the point where we set foot on Downer, I mean the minute we got out of the car, there would be a swarm of cops on it.

Sandy: So what is your interpretation of that? I mean I said that that says a lot, but what is it about Downer vs. Riverwest?

Arno: As far as the police?

Sandy: Right.

Arno: The Downer Avenue Merchants Association went to the police and said we can't have these assholes over here. We want them out of here.

Sandy: Power of cash.

Arno: Rightfully so once again; if I was a business owner I wouldn't want us around either. [laughing]. So that had a lot to do with it. In Riverwest, I don't think at the time there was any—I don't know if there was Riverwest community associations or merchant associations or whatever –entities like that –that would have some sort of dialogue with law enforcement and be able to call them in for a strike.

Sandy: And I think at that time there was ESHAC but they were into housing issues and equity issues.

Arno: Exactly. Not what actually goes on in the street type of thing. So, I guess that's what it came down to. You can't have that in the posh parts of town. If it stays strictly in Riverwest, I don't know how much people would really care.

Sandy: Containment.

Arno: Exactly.

Sandy: So when you dispersed where did you all go?

Arno: We kind of had a repeating pattern when we would disperse. I always had the option of going back home. So that's where I would go—and I hated it there. I would go there only when I had absolutely nowhere else to go. When we got done with Wright Street, we all kind of couch-tripped around and stayed wherever for a couple months and then we got the house on Amy Place on the South side. We all kind of piled in there. I think I was actually on the lease there also. I don't know how I pulled that off, because I don't know who the hell would have leased to me but [laughing]... Amy Place is this obscure little L-shaped street. There is 16th street, and then there's Forest Home and here is whatever this street is, Amy Place was like this, and that's all it is. There is nothing over here, nothing over there. It's in a depressed area also, and it was something we could afford. So that's where we all ended up after a couple months out of the 700 Club. And that's where Pat shot these kids who were doing a drive-by on our house. Uh—which was another couple chapters of the story. Honestly, from that point on, which I would be happy to tell you all you care to know about, but from that point on the only contact we had with Riverwest was when we would occasionally get word of the Baldies living somewhere around there and then we would go back there looking for them. Sometimes we would find them, and sometimes we wouldn't, but that was the only reason we would go back to Riverwest.

Although, in 1990, a really close friend of mine, this kid Chuck from Kenosha... he came from a poorer family that lived in a bad part of Kenosha, and he had a lot of racial conflict in high school. He was kind of second generation Kenosha punk scene. He knew who I was. I didn't really know him though because he started hanging out about the time I left. Chuck was exactly one year younger than me, we had the same birthday. He kind of led and grew his own little crew of skinheads out in Kenosha. Wherever we went we would leave a trail of these horrible flyers with swastikas on them that said "White Power" and had our P.O. box, and he got our address from one of those. He wrote us saying something to the effect of, "What's up? I met Arno before... I am from Kenosha and we have this whole crew." This is probably in 1989, later on after Amy place. Again to the little couchtrip thing, and then we had a house on 23rd and Wells, which was also an adventurous neighborhood. There were constant fights with the locals and whatnot. That's when Chuck first started coming around. We really indoctrinated him and said "Okay, you want to get into white power, this is what's it's all about: here are books to read, this is literature for you to hand out, you get a P.O box –step one." So they did that and we got to be really good friends with them. Chuck was just an awesome kid. He was really—it sounds arrogant to say this following that, but he was a lot like me. He was kinda tall, skinny, dorky, but really charismatic, really funny. He was a great artist, and just a lot of fun to be around. He was the type of person that once you meet him, you don't forget him and you kind of want to be around him. In 1990, we were two houses away from Wells Street. We went from Wells to 23rd and Burnham and then we got a place on 4th and Greenfield. There was a guy we knew who lived in Riverwest—he had a place just him and his girlfriend there. His girlfriend didn't like us coming around there [laughing]. She was like, "I don't want this turning into a skinhead house!" and so there wasn't a whole lot of Riverwest interaction, but once in a while we would go there and hang out. One night Chuck and maybe 3 or 4 of his guys from Kenosha went there to hang out with them, and they went to some—I am not sure what street it was, but here is Humboldt and here is North and there is that big building on the corner. Glaubitz is the guy who lived there with his girlfriend and he had a house over here, and on Humboldt—I don't know if it's still there, but there was a bar there.

Sandy: Past, like further south of North?

Arno: Yeah, south of North Ave towards Commercial or whatever is down there there was a bar over here and Glaubitz and Chuck and his guys went this bar. They were all underage so I don't know how they got served —but they were in there drinking and there were a bunch of Latino gang-bangers in there and they— probably not before too long this conflict arises, they go outside they get in a big brawl and pretty soundly whoop the gang-bangers who then took off. So Glaubitz and Chuck and those guys are all walking back to Glaubitz' street which is that street a block west of Humboldt, whatever that is.

Sandy: Weil.

Arno: It was Weil. The gang-bangers came back. They jumped out of a car from halfway down the block and one of them popped off a couple shots with a .25, one of which went right through Chuck's back and right into his heart and he died on the spot.

And—that was [quiets]—that was the heaviest thing that happened in Riverwest. They never caught the guy. I still to this day feel like they didn't really try very hard. Jim Klisch assures me up and down—you know, that a murder's a murder and they are not going to sweep one under the rug because they don't care about who got murdered—but I don't know if I buy that. I talked to Chuck's mom for the first time in 18 years as I was researching. I got her number from a friend of mind in Racine—a guy we knew from back then and also a good friend of Chuck's—and it took me months to get up the courage to call her. I still feel like it's partly my fault that Chuck was out there with a shaved head and being a skinhead and getting in fights like that. So I—feel that his death is something that's on my shoulders still. I told his mom that, and I am all bawling and she was all bawling, and she put it in perspective. She said, "I went through every 'what if' scenario that could have possibly been 'what if-ed. I mean, what if we didn't move to Kenosha? What if I didn't lose this job here? What if I didn't take this job there? What if I never got divorced? What if one little change in fate's path would have been made somewhere earlier then maybe Chuck wouldn't have gotten killed." She ultimately said it came down to one guy who pulled the trigger and shot him and that's whose fault it is. It's not her fault. It's not my fault. She was just absolutely unbelievably cool about it, and I talked to her a couple of times about just—a lot about Chuck and a lot—we would just started talking about politics or whatever, and it was just really a cathartic thing to go through, but—

Sandy: Did it take any of the weight off?

Arno: Eh—I don't know that it did. It's still something that is really hard for me to deal with. But it just is a part of a broader thing. I deal with a ton of guilt from those days…. it's hard to nutshell this but things escalated from Amy place on. Once—Pat was such a personality.

Sandy: A charismatic leader?

Arno: Exactly—that when he's around, he's the guy. I was always kind of "the guy" too, but I was always kind of in Pat's shadow. And there wasn't any conflict like that —I mean Pat and I were, and still are like brothers.

Sandy: Did he go to prison for shooting—

Arno: He shot the guy at Amy Place, this was years prior to—Amy Place happened in '88 Chuck got killed in 1990, so Pat was already in prison when Chuck was murdered.

Sandy: That's what I was trying to place.

Arno: But what happened at Amy Place was after the Downer riot—when we had moved into Amy Place all the transient skinheads around the country all heard about it and kind of converged here, and we had what we called "Skin Fest" to take on Summer Fest or whatever other fest.

Sandy: Just like African World Festival?

Arno: Yeah! Kind of just like that, only for skinheads. Skin Fest was basically a weekend of—

Sandy: Drunken debauchery?

Arno: Drunken ridiculous beatings, all kinds of horrible things we did, and part of it was on Downer. There was some kind of Downer Street festival going on, so we found our way there and basically started a riot. Everybody there had it up to here with our bullshit and they all attacked us and we fought back, and it was absolute chaos. Some well-known sound guy got his head busted open by one of us—I don't recall who it was—this is according to the newspaper more than my recollection—and after that there was a big story on us in the newspaper. I guess inspired by that story, a bunch of 220 kids from Whitefish Bay high school and their one white friend that lived in Whitefish Bay—I think there were 5 of them—one night they decided they were going to go—according to them, they were just gonna go "see" the skinheads. So they went to Downer, and they found some of the Brew City guys and asked them where we lived. One of them knew, so they told them where we lived, and this is where the story diverges. What Pat said happened, and what everyone at our house said happened—was that those kids came and they slowed their car down in front of our house, and this kid in the passenger seat pulled a pistol out, and he leaned-out to fire on us....

Now—I am leaving out a very important preface to this which happened a week prior to that night. There was a second group of gang squad cops, not Klisch, it was two other ones. And they were nowhere near as nice as Klisch was. They were just self-anointed hardasses who were unapologetically out to take us down. By this time we had been schooled by older skinheads enough to never talk to them. We weren't giving them what they wanted—but in any case they came by when we moved to Amy Place and they said, "You guys know this is gangbanger territory right?" and we were like "Yeah, yeah we figured that out." And they said, "Well, I don't know… but they are gunning for you guys. That's the word on the street is there are going to be some dead skinheads around." This is what the gang squad was telling us. They were telling us, "You guys better watch it. The real gangbangers are after you, and they don't fuck around. They're a real gang." I think it was maybe a day after that, a skinhead from Texas who was staying with us, Hank, was on our front porch and someone took a shot at him with a shotgun from the alley. The majority of the blast hit the side of the house, and you could see all the pellets of birdshot in the aluminum siding, and the rest of it hit Hank in the face, and you could still smell the damn gunpowder when those gang squad cops showed up. They were just instantly there. They said, "What's going on guys?" and we replied, "We just got shot at." And they go "We didn't hear anything." So we say, "Look at the side of the house! That's bird-shot! Someone just shot at us with a shot gun. Look at Hank's face!" Then they looked at Hank's face and they go, "You poked yourself in the face with an ice pick". They were just blatantly, you know—kind of laughing at us. Like, "Oh you guys wanted it, you got it. How do you like it now?" and they are making a point of letting us know they're not gonna to help us. Then they said, "Well maybe someone did shoot at you. I told you the gangsters are after you. There will be more of that so you should just get used to it." And that's kind of how they left it.

So what did we do? We went out and armed ourselves to the teeth. We had an older kind of non-skinhead but racialist friend of ours, a "long hair," if you will—go and buy us a bunch of guns. From that point on, we had 24-hour watches, in every window of the house, where somebody was sitting there with a gun. I remember I worked second shift at Concert Shirt, and I would get off work and I'd come take my watch shift. I would sit on cases of returnable Red, White and Blue, drinking the beer and by the end of my watch I got a case of beer in me and I am sitting there pointing a gun out the window following everyone walking down the street with it, just waiting for someone to give me an excuse to shoot them. It was that frame of mind—that these kids from Whitefish Bay came wandering into. I was at work when this happened, but this car came by, the kid in the passenger seat leaned out with a pistol like this. Pat had a .308 Enfield which is a WWI British bolt-action rifle, and shot him in the shoulder, right here. The way he was shot, the only way he could have been shot there is if he was hanging out the window. Pat fired from the upstairs window and Hank fired a shotgun from the downstairs window and blew all the glass out of the car. A bunch of the kids in the car got shrapnel wounds from the glass, the kid who got shot in the shoulder got pretty messed up. The car went blazing away to St. Mary's on the Eastside, miles away from 16th and Forest Home where the cops ran into them at the emergency room, and arrested them and searched the car and all that stuff, and they didn't have a gun. They had knives, bats, sticks, but they didn't have a gun.

They told the cops they didn't have a gun, and in court they maintained that story. Pat's lawyer was tearing them up. He said, "Why did you guys have bats? Did you think the skinheads had bats?" "Well yeah" "Okay why did you have knives? Did you think the skinheads might have knives?" and "Yeah." "And did you think the skinheads might have guns?" "Oh yeah." "And you didn't bring a gun?" "No, no we didn't have a gun!" I believe firmly that they did have a gun, and to this day, it is somewhere between 16th and Forest Home and St. Mary's on the Eastside. In any case, multiple squads of police were there instantly and they let the car go blazing off. This car full of kids who just got shot, and they didn't pay any attention to them. But they came storming in the house, arrested Pat—he came out there and said, "I shot him. I did it." They arrested Pat, they arrested Hank, and questioned everybody else. They were on us instantly, while letting those kids go driving off. I thought that was awfully strange. There were plenty of squads there. During Pat's trial, it was revealed that these two gang squad guys had rented the upper flat across the street from us, and they were observing us the whole time we were living there—the whole time, except for that night.

They said they took that night off, which also sounds exceedingly strange to me. But that's the story that was given in court. Pat was completely unapologetic. When he testified, he said "That kid pulled a gun out to shoot me and my friends and my house, and that's why I shot him. I shot him in self-defense, I would do it again, and you would probably do the same thing to if someone came by your house with a gun." For that reason Pat got an 8-year sentence and ended up doing 6 in Portage. It was one of those super-hardcore maximum security joints. His son was born when he was in prison, and he didn't get to see him outside of the prison visiting room until he was 6 years old. It was exceedingly bad, it was hard on Pat and his wife, but that's what happened at Amy place. And when Pat—I think that was where we got to when I was talking about.

Sandy: Right, transition and leadership. And escalation you said.

Arno: Yeah. Pat's grandpa bailed him out. So Pat was out for the year between the shooting and the trial and sentencing. And still [laughs]—he's out on $25,000 bail and he is still fighting alongside us, and just being Pat. Bold to the point of being comical, but that's just how he is. So when Pat ended up going away, myself and Will, who was the long-haired guy that bought us the guns at Amy Place—took things over. From that point on, Will and I ran things. Everything that happened up till then was affirming all of the paranoid bullshit that we would be hearing from these racial groups about how the government is out to get us, and it's us against the world and they are going to do all this stuff to shut you down and you know—law means nothing, constitution means nothing, they are going to take you out at all costs. I mean everything that happened to Pat verified that pretty handily in our eyes, at least. All of these things that were happening made me personally really start to believe the premise that the white race was in grave danger, and that there was a genocide going on against us, being perpetrated by a Jewish master plan in which whites would be both violently displaced and simply out-bred. That second part is a fact actually. That's something that I am at peace with right now, but at the time, it was something that was really terrifying for me, because I was in that frame of mind. So when Will and I started running things it was like "this is a movement." We're an organization that's at war with the government. The world is at stake and that's what's on our shoulders. If we don't do something, everything's gone. And I honestly and wholeheartedly believed that. I believed that every flyer I handed out and every kid I brought into that movement, I was doing that for the better—to make this world a better place and to make it a place where my children could grow up. I honestly, honestly believed that. And so did Will, and so did all of the more intelligent people of which there is a surprising amount. A lot of people find that hard to believe but some of the most intelligent people I have ever met were people I knew from back then. Granted, there were plenty of complete psychopaths because racism attracts that sort of element, but I was very wholeheartedly convinced, and that's why when Chuck and other people would come around I would make it my mission to make them feel the same way, and make them have the same passion that I did for my race. That was all I was about for many years. That was my main goal in life. Nowadays I feel horrible about things that I have done personally with my hands, but what I feel most horrible about, and what scares me most is this like unknown quantity of how many—

Sandy: The other kind of violence.

Arno: Yeah. How many people did I bring into that frame of mind, either directly or through someone else? Chuck was a brilliant, charismatic kid, and had he not been brainwashed by me and murdered, who knows what he could have accomplished. People would come to us. It was white kids getting beat up in high school. That was our hugest form of recruiting. Also back then was when Michael McGee was in his heyday and he was making all sorts of noise about sniping whitey from the freeway and just saying all this ridiculous sort of stuff. So you could pretty much throw a rock in Milwaukee and find a disgruntled white person. We would take them aside and say, "Look! This is why it's happening. This is what we have to do." Probably 8 out of 10 of them would be like, "You guys are nuts". But there would be 1 or 2 who would be like, "You know what? You guys would make a lot of sense" and they would come and join our cause. I don't know how many of those people are still like that. I know a lot of them grew up because I am very close with a lot of people who went through that with me. But I don't know how many of them haven't or how many people they recruited so it's like this exponential unknown amount of damage that I did.

On top of that, throughout the whole punk thing and everything else, I was in bands. I started in high school— I was in a band called Stolen Youth and it was funny because it was a straightedge band and I was the most un-straightedge you could be. I was super wasted up there singing about being a straightedge. I took to it. I loved it—I have a really loud voice. I have no singing talent at all, but I can get up there and bellow really loud which is effective for that type of music. Then Pat and I had an Oi! band called One Way, which got a lot of attention. Again the power of music. It was something to gravitate around. Not only do you have this crew and this brotherhood but you've got this band, and you support the band and listen to the music and its almost the lifeblood. Then Pat and I formed another band called Hammerhead, which was Greyhounded out to Napa California by Tom Metzger to play "Aryan Woodstock". We ended up calling it "Aryan Woodflop" cause the feds tweaked some obscure ordinance that stopped us from playing, but we took Cali by storm while we were there—beating up TV cameramen and baldies and gangbangers and whoever else got in our way. The last racial band I had was called Centurion. It was me and a guy from Canada and some other guys from Racine. Got it going in the early 90's. The musicians in the band were really talented and it was much more metal than punk, which was kind of a big deal on the white power music scene at the time because most of the bands up to then had been Oi!-type stuff, and we come out and it's this really hard like Slayer-esque type metal and we were huge! There was a record company called Resistance out of Canada that got investors and was signing white power bands and making CD's and selling them. We were one of the first bands that they signed and the guy who ran it was this absolute —it's funny because record company guys? White power, not white power—all snakes [Both laughing]. But this guy was your stereotypical record company weasel. He was just "Oh, you guys are great! We are going to give you this, this and that! It's going to be so awesome" Telling me, "Buddy you are going to make it!" At the same time we were like money would be nice, but we are doing this for the movement. We want people to listen to our music and be inspired by it—our definition of inspired. We ended up selling over 20,000 CDs around the world over a few years. Centurion was a big thing.

It was ironic because the band was also part of my way out of the whole racial movement in the sense that I had another friend Paul, who left the skinhead scene and he went straight from being a skinhead to being a raver. It's not possible to 180 more than that. He and I were very close so I would hang out with him more and more, and at this time I just wanted to make music. I just wanted to be in a band. As Resistance raked in dough, we began to doubt their sincerity. After giving so much time and energy to the band while raising families and working shit day-jobs, we had gotten really disillusioned about being ripped off, and we were like, "We're just going to make a straight death-metal album with some Viking songs and shit but it's not gonna be overtly racial, and we are going to try to make it big and make this band work." So as we were doing that and my friend Paul was becoming a raver, we started like—and it's— I don't know, this is one of the parts of the story that I don't really like. If I was writing a screenplay or something I wouldn't do it like this, but this is the way it was: me and the guys in the band started smoking pot again. For years —and I mean to this day, amongst skinheads or any kind of white power organization, pot and pretty much anything but alcohol is vehemently forbidden. Reason being—and it makes a lot of sense when you think about it—that typically pot and especially psychedelics are really introspective, and I think in some ways positively mind-altering substances that are just not gonna let you maintain the blinders you have to have on in order to keep this whole racial illusion going. Aside from that, the practical logistics of using marijuana means you are going to be dealing with non-white people at some point to get it. So it was extremely forbidden but I had found out that some of the guys in the band had been smoking pot all along. And I was like "huh" and so I started smoking with them again, and then just instantly starting mellowing out. It gave me a glimpse as to how nice it would be to just give all this stuff up. Paul was our manager, and we let on to him about it. And he was like "what?" and he lets out this huge sigh, because he's been doing it all along too. So everyone kind of comes clean. [laughs] Comes clean with pot use, and we all just start mad tokin' and really from there, it was not a very long journey to the point where I started going to raves with Paul. The first one I went to was on the south side of Chicago and in the most run-down ghetto I'd ever seen. I went down there and it was in this husk of an old roller rink and about 3000 kids of every shade of the rainbow and sexual orientation and everybody is just rocking out and having the best time ever, and it just blew my mind. I was stunned, "I never thought it could be like this." It was really a huge epiphany for me to see that that was possible because I could never imagine that. That's kind of how that band actually ended up leading me out of it.

A bigger factor than that for me though was becoming a single parent. My daughter was born in 1992. Her mother was a skinhead from Chicago. My daughter was conceived because we believed it was our duty to have white children. So after knowing each other for all of 4 months, she had some sort of problem with her IUD and had to have it taken out and we figured, "Well let's have a baby! Duh!" Obviously I am overjoyed that I did; my daughter is the greatest thing that ever happened to me, and she has literally saved my life over and over again. If it wasn't for her I don't know if I would have ever gotten out of that—I would probably be dead or in prison. But, at the time, you know, having a child with someone after being with them for 4 months is not the best course of action—especially when you are both like raging alcoholics and in the midst of this whole skinhead thing. It kind of dooms the relationship.

....so her mother and I split up after not even 2 years. She had two kids from a previous marriage and their dad had taken them down to Key West, so when we broke up, she said "I'm going to take our daughter down to Key West with me." and I replied, "Over my dead body." And she really didn't put up much of a fight so I had our daughter from that point on. The more time I spent with my daughter on my own, I would look back and see what happened and I would think about Chuck and I would think about Pat going to prison and —in 1994 another guy I knew got shot and killed in Racine [clears throat]— it really kind of dawned on me that I didn't want my daughter to ever have to be exposed to that kind of violence—either way: perpetuating it, being a victim of it, whatever. That was truly the driving force behind me leaving. But, if I were to say that pot had nothing to do with it, I would be lying. It was a catalyst.

Sandy: That doesn't surprise me at all.

Arno: And saying that, sometimes I feel it cheapens the whole thing, like "what, so you were this devout racist and then you got high and listened to the Beastie Boys and then you're not?" It's not quite that simple, but in some ways it is. But I mean, it cheapens it in a sense that it's a very stereotypical thing to be laying around stoned listening to music being like, "this is the best music ever", but for me in particular in that moment it was, again, a real epiphany. It was letting those blinders down.

Sandy: I was going to say, it cracks you open if you let it. I don't think it's about getting stupid. I think it's about allowing yourself to connect with yourself and other people.

Arno: Opening yourself up. Right. And the rest of the world. At the same time using marijuana or any other drug does dull the beauty of life —you can't truly experience if you're under the influence of some sort of substance. Nowadays, I still have a lot of goals and aspirations and things I want to do. I'm still always thinking about some great thing that I am going to make happen down the road, and whatever I am doing at the moment is tertiary like whatever, yeah, go fix a computer or whatever. That's what I do for a living by the way. But it's the same kind of thing then, I have always had my head in the clouds, in one cloud or another. But now, I feel like I have a thirst to experience as much of the world and of the Earth and of humanity as I possibly can, and to do so with a clear head. And that I don't think I would have that openness or that kind of broader view if I hadn't have gotten here the way I did.

arno michaelis

appendix B: a comparative review of *Skinhead Confessions* and *Autobiography of a Recovering Skinhead*

In 2007 I sat down and started writing a memoir of my own.

It started with a jot of a sentence. A jot of a memory. Line by line, and not necessarily in chronological order— just things that happened.

As one line memories started to add-up to pages, I tried to flesh out the glimpses of experience into properly sequenced chapters. It became quickly apparent that some sort of corroboration would be necessary if I hoped to proceed, as all too often I was unable to discern detail through the haze of 2 decades; the bulk of which I spent with a blood alcohol content well above the legal limits of all 50 states and territories thereof. From age 14 to 34, I was drunk or hungover much more often than not.

I took inventory of the surprisingly large number of friends formerly considered comrades in a Racial Holy War who had also found the ability to cast hate aside. Our respective immersions in the movement, as well as our individual flights from it, were by no means coincidental. Some of the friends I interviewed were involved before I was, some I had brought in, and others joined completely independent of my influence.

The same holds true for the various ways we left the movement in regards to timing and circumstance. In some cases, their departure may have happened around the same time as mine, but even then it wasn't like we all got together and made a common decision to leave. We all had different influences and different events in our life that led to not only the decision to become white power skinheads, but also the decision to acquiesce to growing out of it.

I sat and talked with very old friends about how they found themselves becoming racists and how they came to abhor racism. While the intent was to shed light on my own booze-soaked inability to recollect, it soon struck me that the more interesting angle beyond a simple linear autobiography was how this group of relatively disparate people all found their way into, and out of, the white racialist movement.

Some of my friends had grown up in poverty. Some had very abusive parents, if there were parents in their life at all. Some came from the kind of tragic dysfunction that you would expect to produce the kind of person who gauges humanity by skin color.

Not so for me. I grew up in a very nice house in a peaceful neighborhood. I went to excellent schools.

While we weren't rich by the standards of the conservative, well-to-do suburb we lived in, we were incredibly wealthy by world standards. I never went hungry or went without shoes on my feet or a shirt on my back. I didn't want for any of the material comforts that literally billions of children across the globe lack at any given moment. My family life wasn't ideal, but then again, I don't think anyone's really is. It's all a relative perspective as to what the hell an ideal family life is. I was hurt and angered by the constant fights over late nights and unpaid bills that poured into our house from a 1.75L scotch bottle. Yet both of my parents loved me dearly.

It certainly couldn't be said that I was neglected. In fact, my earliest memories were filled with affirmation and affection. I was constantly being reminded how smart I was, and how great I was—that I could do absolutely anything I cared to put my mind to. I had all of the positive reenforcement I could handle.

For some reason, that didn't click for me. It actually had a kind of opposite effect. The more my parents and teachers and all of the adults in my life told me how wonderful I was, the more I wanted to be horrible. My self image was an antonym of who they expected me to be. As I grew older, my relationship with the world became increasingly violent and careless, despite the love and positive reenforcement that my family had showed me.

Comparing my childhood to the sometimes horrific

experiences of my peers, it occurred to me that I had no excuse for how I turned out. But is there ever an excuse to become someone who would attack another human being because of the color of their skin? I don't believe that there is. Every one of us has the ability to react to the world around them with compassion instead of aggression. That decision invariably lies with the individual and there's no amount of bad treatment that can justify perpetuating aggression.

Yet according to probability, it's known that children who are victims of violence are much more likely to become adults who victimize others. Reading memoirs from other former skinheads adds to the evidence I've collected to reenforce this truth.

Front and center are the books *Skinhead Confessions* by T.J. Leyden and *Autobiography of a Recovering Skinhead* by Frank Meeink.

Googling "former skinhead" produces T.J.'s blog, StrHATE Talk. T.J.'s name is familiar to me. I remember hearing it back when I was involved with the movement, but I never met or interacted with him—at least not that I recall. T.J. is from California and was very active on the West coast recruiting and organizing racist skinheads.

My one foray out that way was in 1989 for a white power music festival called "Aryan Woodstock". My band Hammerhead was supposed to play, and we rolled round-trip from Chicago to San Francisco on a Tom Metzger-financed Greyhound ride, along with a small entourage who had managed to scrape-up the $99 each to join us. We ended up having 16 skinheads on a 52 hour each-way bus ride. Once we got out to Napa, the local government leveraged an ordinance loophole that barred us from playing music, though we were still allowed to gather. In true Aryan Warrior fashion, the only reasonable course of action was to get royally shitfaced and commence beating the hell out of hotel rooms and each other. The debacle is know to this day by racists and otherwise as "Aryan Woodflop".

While I was out there I did meet a lot of West coast movement honchos, many of whom were mentioned in *Skinhead Confessions*. T.J. was not among them, as he was enlisted in the marine core at the time, where he was stationed in Hawaii and actively recruiting from his barracks.

Reading T.J.'s book as I was writing my own during the summer of 2008 sent me reeling with simultaneous reflection and disparity. I turned pages in *Skinhead Confessions* that vividly described things that had happened to me, rages that were felt, and regret that still aches. Considering the evident parallels between T.J.'s path and my own, my connection with his book isn't surprising. But the story itself and the lesson it delivers has a universal quality that engages all readers—ex-skinheads or otherwise.

Former Philadelphia skinhead Frank Meeink was also a contemporary of mine and very active on the East coast, recruiting there and leading his own gangs of skinheads in a series of racial assaults. After being sent to prison for the vicious kidnapping and beating of a suspected anti-racist, his change of heart began as he became friends with people he had sworn to hate.

As it was with T.J., I strained to recall if I had ever met Frank. After reading his book *Autobiography of a Recovering Skinhead*, I learned that we not only shared a history of racism and redemption, but also that Frank had taken substance abuse above and beyond even the extremes that I had. The two of us could very well have had long conversations lost to mutual blackouts, although after talking with Frank recently, we were able to agree that we hadn't met back in the day.

What we could also agree on was how imperative it was that we shared our stories with the world in hopes of helping others avoid falling into the reeking mire of hate and violence. Frank and co-author Jody M. Roy did an incredible job of recreating his life with reality and thoroughness, which I can attest to having a familiarity with the skinhead landscape of the late 80s and early 90s. *Autobiography of a Recovering Skinhead* is one of the most immersive and poignant books I've ever read, and I've read quite a bit for 35 years or so now.

Examining my own life, along with the lives of T.J. Leyden, Frank Meeink, and the lives of all the friends I've interviewed, it is plain to see that we were all very angry teenagers who embraced angst like it was all that we had in the world. There is a certain personality type that demands living a life where boundaries aren't set by society but by the individual. It's an outlook where making your own rules seems as natural as breath. There's nothing inherently evil about that type of personality; it's the same mindset that has spawned scientific discoveries and schools of thought that have made the Earth a much nicer place to live. Great heros and heroines throughout human history have all shared a dissatisfaction with the status quo and the will to do something about it. Anti-fascists during the Spanish Civil war and WWII, as well as activists of the Civil Rights and anti-war movements were all inspirational examples of rebels who refused oppression and organized against it.

But when that kind of person makes certain mistakes in certain circumstances, things as atrocious as the aforementioned things were wonderful can be set as in motion. Just as Buddha, Jesus of Nazareth, the Prophet Muhammad, Mohandas Karamchand Gandhi, and Dr. Martin Luther King, Jr. were all examples of people who made their own rules and who had a positive impact on society, there is unfortunately a perhaps even longer list of people who had horrific impacts on the world—stemming from that same core need to dictate reality and motivate others.

Frank, T.J., and myself were all dissatisfied teenagers who decided to make our own rules. The question to ask is; if we could've followed in the footsteps of either MLK or Adolph Hitler, what caused us to go one way or another?

The answer lies in part with how we chose to react to our family lives, or in some cases the complete lack thereof. Via Life After Hate, I've written in some depth about how I reacted to my family situation while I was growing up. Frank Meeink had the most negative experience of the three of us in that both of his parents were utterly absentee or at best apathetic because of a deeply rooted and seemingly insurmountable chain of addiction. As a young child, he suffered horrible physical abuse at the hands of his stepfather. By the time he encountered the skinhead movement, he was a feral teen; fending for himself, with no parental involvement whatsoever.

T.J. Leyden's early home life seemed to have fallen somewhere in-between that of myself and Frank. His parents had been divorced by the time he was a teenager, but the time before and after was rife with alcohol-inspired violence. While T.J.'s mother made genuine and repeated attempts to foil his involvement in the movement, his relationship with his father was strained by booze and the distance it brings. The resulting tension between his parents was a constant source of pain in T.J.'s life.

Not one of us had a mom and dad who were happy and in love with each other. While my house wasn't technically a broken home—my parents didn't get divorced until I was 18—I grew up wishing that it was. My mom and dad stayed together in a vain effort to provide some sort of stability for my brother and I, but their constant fighting ultimately destabilized things to the point where I felt an overwhelming need to get as far away from them as possible and smash everything I could in the process. Though Frank and T.J.'s parents were divorced when they were much younger, the end result of flight and rage remained.

The three of us grew up in households as wildly different and as far apart lifestyle-wise as they were were far apart geographically, yet we all became exceedingly violent and hateful leaders who caused a significant amount of harm to innocent people; not only with our own hands, but more catastrophically through the people we recruited into the movement, and the people that they recruited, and so-on.

Another commonality that's very apparent in all three of our cases is substance abuse. T.J. and myself both abused alcohol with reckless abandon. Frank took dependency giant-steps farther after he left the movement, when drinking had lead to prescription painkillers which ultimately led to heroin, where he found a definition of rock-bottom that T.J. and I have thankfully never known. All three of us leveraged alcohol in the recruiting process. Inflating our already-rampant egos with beer, we took on a larger-than-life aspect as prospective skinheads were fed beer themselves until we appeared as mythic heros to revere and emulate. Drunkenness was a prime means of disconnect from basic human goodness that could have brought about earlier turnarounds if not headed-off the racism and violence all together.

I'm very happy to say that all three of us have taken steps to address the substance abuse in our lives. Addiction is a horror that can never be completely conquered. Once whatever substance takes control, the shadow of relapse is forever cast. Every day requires a conscious effort to not only react compassionately instead of violently, but also to do so with as clear a head as possible. As low as we have all respectively sunk, we've made great strides from where we were and the three of us no longer drink. That has been a metamorphic and catalytic step as we've moved from being activists for hate to being activists for peace.

There are a host of similarities in regard to our lifestyles and approaches during the time we were involved in the movement. All three of us recruited by inflaming already-tense racial situations in high schools and colleges. We would seek out brewing conflict between white kids and everyone else then ensure the explosion of said conflict by littering campuses with white power flyers. This reliably produced a scenario where people involuntarily on our side had to choose between joining up with us or getting their ass kicked.

Music was also imperative to not only the recruiting process, but also to the building and maintenance of the racial dogma that drove us to hurt people. Each one of us was initially drawn to the skinhead counterculture by the polarizing and energizing hate rock that it revolved around. As evidenced by our disparate locations and the ongoing activity of white power skinheads and other racist organizations, these common threads of music and related recruiting strategies are much more a constant of the movement rather than particular manifestations of our individual personalities.

The crux of the common story that is relayed through so many different lenses is reached when we describe how we respectively came to realize how wrong we were. Each of us experienced a unique chain of events that led to the same turnaround, but the most powerful factor in setting racism aside was that we all really started to feel a pressing need to do so shortly after we became fathers.

T.J.'s first open defiance of hate came at a skinhead party where children were gathered to attack a piñata fashioned to look like a lynched black man. He couldn't watch his son take part in that symbolic hate crime. The realization of what was in store for his little boy hit him with exponentially more force than the Louisville Slugger the kids were given to batter the effigy could possibly have. T.J.'s own life had gone to such miserable shit after years of involvement in the movement; would his son even survive long enough to have sons of his own having been born into it?

As Frank's doubt had already began to percolate, initiated by his friendship with blacks and Latinos in prison, he saw news footage of wounded children being carried away from the wreckage of the Oklahoma City bombing in 1995. The thought of his own daughter being killed or maimed inspired an empathy for human beings that transcended the racial dogma he had imposed upon himself. Both T.J. and Frank seized those moments—or perhaps the moments seized them—to find the courage necessary to not only leave the movement, but to begin a compassionate opposition to hate that they've been actively engaged in since the mid-nineties.

crazy love and respect out to:

Julie Sanders!!

My Aunts and Uncles and Cousins. Pam B. The Miller Family. My sisters Angie Aker and Tanya Cromartie and their families. Rob Hasselkus. Bashir Malik and his Family. The O'Malley Family. Skully. Nancy, Bill (RIP), John, and Black Dragon Tattoo. Sammy, Denise, and the Rangel Family. The Kaleka Family. Paul Urbanek. The Welland Family. Larry Hisle, Jr. Jim Flint. The Kaplan Family. The Carpenter Family. The Puerling Family. The Katz Family. The Dykstra Family. The Kinyon Family. Paul and his dad. Christian Picciolini. The Armstrong Family. The Stehlik Family. The Loos Family. Banta. Elya. Lenore. Zephyr. Woody. Chris and Sarah. Jody and Savanna. All my friends I grew up with in Da Q.

Brain, Mike McQueen, Hippie Pat, and all of the 700 Club denizens. Clayton. Maria. Tom G. Leslie. Jason. Jon, Bill, and all the OG West Bend crew. Dave O. Dan and Rush-Mor Records. All my punker friends who I turned my back on, especially Don and Dean Dirt (RIP). Dave Dred. Beautiful Burt. JJ. Everyone from the eternal Keno-Core scene. Jim Klish. Chuck Fuckemup. Brass Tacks and Crew. Tom and Tanya. George Burdi. Tony Mac. Dave. Brett.

Bill And Wendy and their girls. Matt & The Massive Posse. Kurt and Drop Bass Network. DJ Fishead. All my

MW-RAVES people. Everyone from the Gabber List. Bekka Rekka Roller Skates. Angelus and Tex Bailey and their Fam. Kari, Andrew, and Emery. Nick, Allison, and Ella. Sharifah. Larry. Deva. Berry. Mark. T-Dawg. Shain. X-tina. Bacon Management. Mike P. Kevin Unibomber. Josh Anonymous. Dan, Tina, and their little girl. Johnny, Tanya and fam. The Stugard Family. Audrey and Dea. Sam, Ben, Adam, and Lucy. Aaron, Abby, and fam. Devin. Emily. Franjo. Joey and Shelly. Dan and JulieAnn. Dawn and Jeff and boys. Jon K. Jon Gotti. Dylan. Lia. Melissa L. D Money. Quinn. Eyebrow. Markie and Sarah. Nichole D. Jeremiah. Abe. Tim. Alan C. Brett O. Zach and Ben E. All the MW-Hardcorps. Adam Z. Eric M. and all my monkeys at MPC. Pidd and Nidd. Sgt. Clueless. Cueball. Dan S. All the guys I used to play hockey with.

Everyone I've ever got stupid drunk with and don't remember.

Alan Heyn, Berni Xiong, Beverly Kipp, Brain Mahany, Doctori Sadisco, Jeb Platt, Judith Ford, Julienne Marlaire, Katharina Hren, Michelle Daniels, Michelle Jones, Natali Huess, Nathaniel Holton, Pam Nanet, Tamara Westfall, Terry Hoffman-Vincevineus, The Bus Bandit, Theresa Nickol, Zek J Evets, Callen Harty, Carlos Eduardo de Oliveira Ramalho, Christopher Sofolo, Kipp Efinger, Gregory and Malissa Chambers, Jo Berry, Joel A. Brown, Jonathan Moore, Mike Frontier, Mubin Shaikh, Ornella Umubyeyi, Paul Kendel, Robi Damelin, Rosalyn Boyce, Shaun Jacob, Tahir Malik, Jason Mueller, Umme Thara,

Charles Ryder, Daniel Gallant, Jack Varnell, Daylee Iris Bree, Emma Zeldin, Harjit Singh, Harvey Taylor, James Zarate, Jessica Cagle-Fillion, Laura Gonzalez, Marina Cantacuzino, Miguel Lewis, Sahar Shahin, and Sayra Mobeen.

All my Summer of Peace brothers and sisters!

Brian, Callen, Sol, and everyone at Proud Theater!

Evie. Manny G. and Family. Marsha. Zebra Panel. Rick and Yuki. Kim K. All my Turners climbing fam. Will Fellows. Bronze. Earl Ingram and Chez at 1290AM. Anthony Courtney and everyone at Coffee Makes You Black. Ellie B-D. Everyone at Beans & Barley. Everyone at EE-Sane. Everyone at Ouzo Cafe. Everyone at Singha Thai. Alterra. Vladka. Dan and Sonya and their girls. Chester Steve and fam. Carly, Abby, Charlie, Iesha, and everyone else from Dr. Kailin's classes. Dr. Julie Kailin. Amber Miller and everyone at WWBIC. Dimitry. Holly B. Carolyn W. Lydia E. Erika, Alex and Mamma's Eggrolls. Connie Littlefield. Chosen Few Gym. Ronnie. Dustin Zarnikow and The UWM Post. Lisa Kaiser and The Shepherd Express. Emilio and everyone at ACLU Wisconsin. Jeff Kelly-Lowenstein. Jonathan S. and all my FHL possee. Jose S. Monica, Tracy, Annie, Julia, and all of the other wonderful Yoga teachers I've had. Wild Space Dance Co. Yvette L. Alan A. Julio G. Sarah and TRUE Skool. The Flobots. David and The Urban Underground. Noah, Ava, and all our Public Allies. Change.org. Milwaukee Turners. Milwaukee Public Theatre. Students and staff at Milwaukee College Prep.

Lake Valley Camp. Josh Brandsgaard. Jen B. Shanon Magnani. Francisco Garibay. Wyndy Jaz and her mom. Zach Stoner. Adam and the Rusty Ps. Douglas H. Every single one of my Facebook friends—there are too many of you to list but I love you all!

Jeff and Jeri. Jerry U. Joel C. Ben J. Karen. Kathy. Eva. Matt. Brett and Family. Everyone at the COU. Britt. Larry and Sabrina and Family. Everyone at the MBA. Barry, Leslie, and Family. Ray and Tina. Margret and the BWVSLLC crew. All of my clients. All my BigChain people. Tor Furumo. Christina Garza-Nelson and the coolest Sociology class ever. Megan Borpsy Orpsy Noskoviak and her mom. Andi White and Badger High School. EJ and Megan. Kim Stetz. Annika Lundkvist. Amy Ferris. Thomas Hellstrom.

Everyone at Google, the CFR, Tribeca Films, and all of my brothers and sisters in the AVE network. The Forgiveness Project. Trevor Sacco and everyone at GenNext. Community Boost Consulting. Life After Hate Magazine Editor-in-chief Angela King. Mike Abramson. Jeff, Malissa, and Abe Winkowski. Dannielle and Kristin Everyone Is Gay. Penn State International Center for the Study of Terrorism. Everyone at Cascade and Pacific Academies. Father Greg Boyle and everyone at Homeboy Industries. Serve2Unite. The Sikh Temple in Oak Creek WI.

Cudahy High School!

B-Boys and B-girls everywhere!

T.J. Leyden and Frankie Meeink, for leading the way and for being my friends.

Laura, Preston, Sarah, and Michael.

Everyone who has listened to me. Everyone who reads this. Each one of you helps me heal and together we can make the world a more peaceful and compassionate place.

For endless inspiration: Jesus. Frederick Douglass. W.E.B. Du Bois. Mohandas Karamchand Gandhi. Dr. Martin Luther King Jr. Satwant Singh Kaleka. Clarence Kailin. Bruce Lee. Piers Anthony. Stephen King. Hunter S. Thompson. Neal Stephenson. The Beastie Boys. Run-DMC. Céu. CLUTCH. The Clash.

My Sangha.

Shambhala.

The Buddha.

and I still feel like I forgot someone...

arno michaelis

about the author:

Father, Son, Brother, Author, Speaker, Listener, Teacher, Student, Adventurer, Practitioner. Imperfect mistake-maker and perpetual lesson-taker. Truly experiencing my path and loving it more with each step.. Enjoys climbing things and warm saltwater. Cold saltwater is kinda nice too.

You just read the rest.

...or did you?

arno michaelis

mylifeafterhate.com

75898169R00134

Made in the USA
Columbia, SC
25 August 2017